SISTER SALTY
Sister Sweet

A MEMOIR OF
SIBLING RIVALRY

by SHANNON KRING BIRÓ &
NATALIE KRING

RUNNING PRESS
PHILADELPHIA · LONDON

9   8   7   6   5   4   3   2
Digit on the right indicates the number of this printing

Library of Congress Control Number: 2006934602

ISBN-13: 978-0-7624-2922-6
ISBN-10: 0-7624-2922-4

Cover and interior design by Joshua McDonnell
Cover Photography by Pier Nicola D'Amico
Typography: Cheltenham, Brush Script, and Goudy

This book may be ordered by mail from the publisher.
Please include $2.50 for postage and handling.
But try your bookstore first!

Running Press Book Publishers
2300 Chestnut Street
Philadelphia, PA 19103-4371

Visit us on the web!
www.runningpress.com

For Kayla

Behold, the Only Thing Greater Than Myself

Shannon, age 4

THE NIGHT OF MY SISTER'S BIRTH, Mom and Dad went to the hospital without me, leaving me with my maternal grandmother and a new Play-Doh Fuzzy Pumper Barbershop.

As was customary whenever I left the house, I brought along my red suitcase with white stitching. I took great pleasure in filling it with anything I could get my hands on—spaghetti noodles, lint-laced pocket change, wilted dandelions. I especially liked bringing my suitcase to my grandmother's trailer, where a dazzling array of Avon bells and perfume bottles shaped like cars and Bo Peep beckoned from the particleboard hutch that was the focal point of her tiny living room. When I'd eye my mark—a blue glass bottle shaped like a guitar, say, or a southern belle with a parasol and a park bench molded to her thigh—my grandmother, whom I called Gabby and my father simply referred to as Nutcase, would shimmy and say, "Oooh, she's like her Gabby. She likes nice things! Oooh, yes she does." And I did. I got my love of German cars and large diamonds from Gabby, despite the fact that she drove a rusted sky-blue Ford Fairlane and got her biggest piece of bling from the Home Shopping Network.

That night, we played cards. My 12-year-old Uncle Jeff positioned me in front of the dining-room mirror so he could watch my hand, while Gabby watched his in the UFO-shaped brass chandelier. Papa, my grandfather, didn't play and instead sucked his pipe and clicked across the faux hardwood floors in his shiny black ankle boots. Despite his sixth-grade education, Papa was an engineer at a paper mill and got free toilet paper. He was also the lead guitarist in a country-western band that made records. He smiled only when drinking Schlitz, watching John Wayne or boxing on TV, or speaking with one of his lady friends Gabby described as "dirty two-timing whooores." That night, he wore the strained expression of a man not accustomed to being with his family.

Gabby said Papa was always too busy cabareting around town to come home and treat her right. "He thinks this is a goddamned hotel!" she'd complain. "He only comes home to eat, shower, and pet that dirty *assle.*" The dirty assle in question was Papa's poodle, Chewy, who had one drippy, blind eye and cowered behind Papa's recliner whenever Papa wasn't home. Gabby was as jealous of Chewy as she was the dirty two-timing whooores and took every opportunity to "show him who's boss." Once, when Chewy brushed past her white pant leg, Gabby punched him in the throat so hard that the dog flew halfway across the room and landed splat on the coffee table. Another time, when letting him in from outside, she slammed him in the screen door and cackled like a cartoon witch.

I didn't understand why Gabby wanted Papa to be home more, because when he was, all they did was fight. Friday and Saturday nights were the worst.

Papa would come home from work to shower, spritz himself with cologne, and go to his closet to pick out one of the many rope-decorated shirts with his name printed neatly on the tags of each in black magic marker. Each of Papa's non-fabric possessions had "Orv" or "Orville D." scratched into it with his pocketknife or burned into it with the pointy tool I coveted. Many of these objects were locked in metal boxes—the padlocks and boxes also marked, of course—that he soldered together himself. The back of his closet was full of these boxes, and I'd work on opening them for hours sometimes, aggravated that my tools—Gabby's plastic hair pick and a spatula—were insufficient for the job.

"You iron my shirt?" Papa would ask, examining whatever shirt he'd selected.

"What do you mean, did I iron the damn thing?" Gabby would snap. "Look at it!"

"It ain't ironed! I can't wear this!"

"I pressed it, you damn idiot! Look at it! Just look!" she'd yell, ripping the neatly pressed shirt out of his hand. No matter how much starch she used, Gabby's ironing was unsatisfactory.

As Gabby got out the ironing board, Papa would go back to the bathroom, where he'd make three waves in the top of his damp, white-blonde hair. After tapping his comb—simply stamped "Orv"—on the edge of the sink, he'd reach for Gabby's Aqua Net. At this point, he'd close the bathroom door. Papa hairsprayed in private, a habit Gabby called "Saturday night shame" and used as an excuse to pick another fight.

"You hear that?" she'd ask, pressing her ear to the door to hear the aerosol hiss. "That damn fool is using my Aqua Net! Go on! A man using Aqua Net. Who ever heard of such a thing! Arlene said her Norb would never use hairspray! Never!"

"Get the hell away from the door and iron my shirt, woman!" Papa would snipe.

"You hear how he talks to me? Like I'm mud! Mud! Arlene, that fat slob, she don't even keep herself up nice! She don't even perm her hair, and her Norb, he treats her like a queen." Gabby's scream turned to a stage whisper and she added, "Three months. Three months he ain't come 'round me. Arlene says Norb would *never* go that long. No way. He comes 'round her all the time." I didn't know what Gabby was talking about; Papa had to walk past her every time he had to shower, even though I was sure he'd rather not.

That night, I stole a couple of glances at Papa and then went back to ignoring him, as he ignored me. I was secretly thankful for his presence, because Mom didn't allow me to stay alone with Gabby.

When I tired of cards, I got out my paper and markers and worked on whatever book I was writing and illustrating at the time. I learned to read and write at a very early age, getting tripped up only by the letter W, which I sometimes found impossible to stop. "Down up, down up," Mom would remind me as I down upped, down upped, down upped my way across the entire page and often onto to the table before throwing a fit and tearing the paper into confetti. Because Mom deemed staplers dangerous, I had my own hole punch and would bind the pages on which I achieved perfect W's with colorful yarn pinched from Gabby's knitting drawer.

When I finished working on my book, I got out the Fuzzy Pumper Barber Shop, sniffing the various tubs of Play-Doh and fighting the temptation to eat them. Each time the phone rang, we'd race to it, Gabby pushing me out of the way in her mad dash. As I cranked out salty blue hair, across town Mom cranked out Natalie, who, it was reported by Uncle Jerry (who had been there when she was born), had rosy cheeks and dark brown hair like my dad's.

"Oooh, I bet they named her after Natalie Woods," Gabby speculated after she'd hung up, pronouncing Natalie as "Nadly," like she always did. "Dark hair just like her daddy and Natalie Woods. Oooh, she'll be beautiful, not like her mother."

My heart sank, knowing Natalie's looks alone could cost me my standing with Gabby. She once told me she hated Mom because she had Papa's same dishwater blonde hair, pasty, ghost-white skin, and freckles that look like dirt. "Oooh, I can't stand looking at your ma," she said, patting her own hair, which was black and wiry like her mother's had been, and streaked with auburn like the girl's on the Clairol box, her scalp and hairline often bearing the same shade. "Makes me sick. She looks just like that dirty, dirty assle!"

I never understood how my own light complexion didn't make Gabby hate me. And though I didn't know who Nadly Woods was, I added her to the growing list of grown-ups I was angry at:

Mom

Dad

Uncle Jerry

Gabby

Papa

Nadly Woods

Each offender had wronged me in the same way: They'd been excited—happy even!—about the interloper who set up shop in Mom's stomach. Even Jerry, Mom's younger brother and Jeff's older brother, shared in the joy.

Jerry had recently moved out of our house. Three years earlier, when he was 14 and Gabby and Papa moved to the trailer, he came to live with us so that he didn't have to change schools. Jerry had the same sad, far-off eyes as Mom and quickly became my best friend. He played *Land of the Lost* and *Star Trek* with me whenever I told him to. He took me fossil hunting and taught me about Orion's Belt. On Easter, he threw me a party at which we sang songs, blew on paper horns, hunted for brightly colored Easter eggs, and danced around the piles of party favors and presents he'd wrapped in pink paper and ribbons. I liked my Easter party so much that he didn't even make me wait until the next year to have another one. All I had to do was frown and it was Easter all over again!

Sometimes Jerry got scared and couldn't play. Mom would give him a brown paper bag and tell him to put his head between his legs. She'd touch his hair like she did mine when I puked and told him everything was going to be okay. When he was all better, I'd draw him a picture. Now there would be a baby who would want to play with *my* Jerry, to sing "Shannon 'n Little Peter Cottontail" and look at stars.

"What'd they name her?" Papa asked.

"Nadly. Oooh, it's beautiful."

"Madeline?" he asked.

"No, Nadly, you damn idiot!"

"MADELINE?" Papa only had a hearing problem where Gabby was concerned. I didn't bother to correct him, and for the rest of his life, Papa called my sister Madeline.

A few months into Natalie's invasion of our home, Mom and Dad got to worrying that she might be retarded or deaf because she was so quiet and mild-mannered next to how I was at her age. Mom would hang brightly colored pictures beside her crib, pointing at them and exclaiming enthusiastically, "Look Natalie. Look at the bright colors!" No response. With worry lines on her forehead, Mom would crank up Natailie's mobile. "Look at the pretty mobile Natalie! Up here, Natalie!" She'd snap her fingers to get Natalie's attention, and again, no response. Soon, Natalie's mobile was replaced with a larger, faster, noisier version that she ignored just the same.

As an infant, I would flash a Gerber-baby smile one moment and the next scream until my skin mottled. Mom would dance around me in a panic, offering comforting words or a song while worrying that I was hungry, had my head positioned wrong, or had come down with a bout of Typhoid fever.

I have been told that when I was just three months old, I could no longer be placed in my baby seat while Mom did housework or I'd kick my legs and propel myself across the table or floor. Prop a rattle in the side of Natalie's baby seat, and she'd blink at it for hours. At three-and-a-half months, I screamed so hard that Mom feared I'd pop the blood vessels in my face. Picking me up made me scream harder, so she summoned the advice of the family doctor, a Filipino, who, despite having been transplanted to Wisconsin's Northwoods several years earlier, instructed her, "baby leave go crib." So I was left in my crib, where I writhed around with determination on my face for three hours, until I rolled over and at last fell asleep with a contented smile. Natalie never cried, an occasional squeak the only indication that she was hungry or needed a diaper change. It turned out she wasn't retarded or deaf, but that didn't stop me from telling her she was when she was old enough to understand what it meant, adding that she was adopted for good measure.

Saying mean things to Natalie quickly became my favorite pastime. Mom's new half-hour afternoon nap afforded me this opportunity.

"Bring your toys up on the bed and play while Mommy and Natalie sleep," Mom would say, long having given up on my napping with her. I'd play tea party or house until Mom drifted off, and then I'd throw down my stuffed animals and slink to Natalie's bassinette.

"You're an ugly baby," I'd whisper into my sleeping sister's ear. "I hate you, and I wish you'd go away!" Soon, potshots were replaced with imaginary gunshots, as I began playing "the Stuffy-Fluffy shooting game."

Borne of my sick cat having to be shot, and of the many Sunday afternoon hunting shows played on the local TV station, the Stuffy-Fluffy shooting game involved my giant stuffed bunny and me rendezvousing at various secret locations to plan our attacks on baby stuffed animal prey. With Mom's first snore, I'd grab my pink broom gun and Bristle Block walkie-talkie and whisper into it, "Stuffy, I'll meet you at the staircase at two o'clock. I hear Miss Panda's baby was spotted in the kitchen."

No matter what I thought, though, everyone loved the "well-behaved baby"—grocery store clerks, bank tellers, my own mother. They showered her with nonsensical jabber and she flashed them her shiny pink smile in return.

"Mom, look what I can do," I'd yell whenever she gave Natalie attention. I'd quickly hop, whistle, recite the "Pledge of Allegiance"—anything that stood a chance of dazzling her enough to forget this baby business.

"Wow, good job," Mom would say without looking up from Natalie. She was always staring adoringly at Natalie and cooing over how beautiful she was. (Years later, I would learn that Mom had locked herself in the bathroom and cried when I was born, because I looked like her.) "But be careful not to cartwheel too close to your sister's swing."

Dad was equally enthralled with Natalie. Once, on a commercial break during the miniseries *Roots,* I walked in the kitchen and found him taking a just-bathed Natalie from the sink. He held her high above his head and proclaimed, "Behold! The only thing greater than yourself!"

At that moment, Dad confirmed what I'd pretty much already realized. Shortly thereafter, I took up ripping the knobs off of the television and stereo and playing with matches. I drank the entire bottle of my sister's Baby Tylenol and tried putting a pinch of my dad's Copenhagen snuff between my cheek and gum. I even started cussing, calling my new cat a "cocksucky" when she wouldn't let me put barrettes in her hair.

It became clear that only a certain amount of goodness was distributed between Natalie and me, and apparently she got it all.

Bathroom Habits of an Unchallenged Genius

Shannon, age 5

I couldn't stop peeing.

This was the latest in a long line of compulsions: popping my left shoulder in and out of socket seven times each and every time I became aware of its presence. Carrying objects with my elbows so as not to get germs on my hands. Being unable to go to sleep until I had noted which song was playing on every radio station. This last compulsion presented two major problems: 1. I had Uncle Jerry's old shortwave radio and therefore dozens of stations, and 2. By the time I got to the end of the dial, new songs had started on the preceding channels. I also felt it necessary to touch every object in stores that I may never visit again, such as zoo gift shops, especially if the objects were expensive and accompanied by "You break it, you buy it!" warnings. On field trips to museums,

I was not only compelled to jump over or limbo under the ropes but also to lick the works of art once I got in. But my peeing was a new problem, an all-consuming one that rendered my other compulsions mere hobbies.

Like everything else that caused the smile to leave my face, my urination marathon greatly disturbed Mom.

"Does it hurt? Does it hurt before you pee?" she'd ask me each time I ran to the bathroom, which seemed like every ten seconds.

"No," I answered, closing the bathroom door with my elbow.

"Does it hurt while you pee? Tell Mama if you have an owie when you pee." I could hear from her shallow breathing on the other side of the door that she was becoming more frantic.

"No," I said, carefully lining the toilet seat with toilet paper.

Mom was scooting me out the door to the doctor's office before I'd finished my first round of hand washing. It was fine with me that I had to go in. I loved the strong-smelling soap at the clinic, and the nurses who always gushed about how pretty I was.

It was on that particular visit to the clinic that Mom learned from our doctor, "Infection no problem. Stress child in head." This diagnosis sent Mom straight to her bookcase, which was crammed with titles such as *I'm OK-You're OK, Born to Win: Transactional Analysis with Gestalt Experiments* (which she called her bible), and *T.A. for Tots.*

It was from these books that Mom and Uncle Jerry derived their secret language, which relied heavily on the whispering of terms such as "pig parent," "intrapsychic disturbances," and "games." It seems Mom didn't want to "suppress" or "scar" my "ego," which to me meant only that I could freely throw tantrums. So long as I didn't physically harm myself or anyone else, anything was fair game and resulted in extra playtime, cuddling, and store-bought treats. When screaming "I hate you!" became my sole method of communication, however, Mom made me an appointment with her psychotherapist.

The day of my first session, I wore gummy-soled Mary Janes, new brown cords, and my most demure smile. Mom wore her hair parted down the middle, which indicated to me that the day would not be a good one.

Mom had recently started seeing this shrink. I blamed him for her crying when she looked out the window or took a bath, for her pushing my father away when he tried to hug her. On the rare occasions when she slept now, Mom would do so in her clothes, shoes, and glasses, awakening like a frightened kitten at the slightest noise.

There were other reasons for my predisposed hatred for the shrink. Not only did he teach Mom to put me in the corner (Kring dining room wallpaper circa 1978: fifty-four blue paisleys down the corner, eighteen hideous yellow flowers on the bias), but also to twist my arm behind my back when I started kicking the radiator and tearing down the wallpaper.

It was the same story every evening before dinner. "But Kerry! She won't stop and I will break her arm! Look at how far it's bent already!" This was usually followed by Mom saying she didn't want to be like Gabby. By the way she said it, being like Gabby would be worse than being a pig parent.

"Then I guess you'll break it," Dad would answer without looking up from the evening news.

Once I was alone in his office, the shrink made me sit on the floor. I tried not to think about all of the feet that had been where I was sitting. I'd recently stopped my three-year habit of carrying objects with my elbows, but I now refused to remove my shoes unless I'd constructed a safety path of coloring book pages or newspapers. Foot germs were the worst.

"I hear you're a wonderful artist," he said slowly. His mouth was a line, but the crinkles beside his eyes betrayed him. "I'd like you to draw a picture of your family."

He had only crayons, no markers, and the carpet would make my strokes too broad and clunky, possibly even cause the thin, brownish paper to tear.

"May I please have a book to write on?" I asked, lowering my head and batting my eyelashes.

"Why, certainly. What good manners you have. You're very well-behaved," he lied. Surely, Mom had told him the truth. *Maybe this guy wasn't so bad,* I thought. He was a pretty good liar.

I purposely conjured up a cheery-looking scene, beginning with Mom, whose hair I drew parted sharply to the left in Laser Lemon. Next, I drew Dad, equal in height to Mom. Then I added a smiling sun, black V's for birds, Natalie swaddled in our father's embrace, and finally me with a big grin. I threw in a house with two windows, a door, and a purposely lopsided brick chimney. It was the sort of crap other kids my age drew and did not at all resemble reality.

The shrink looked pleased with my work and chatted a bit about my interests, Barbies and playing outside and drawing and paper dolls. I chose not to tell him that I played *60 Minutes* with my favorite Barbie and that I had illustrated stretch marks on her with a Sharpie. Her shiny hair would always flop back to a center part, even though I did my best to keep it off to the side.

"You'll be able to play with your sister when she gets a bit older," the shrink said, leaning forward in his chair. "That will be fun, won't it?"

"Yes." Mom kept saying the same thing, and it did sound fun, but for now Natalie couldn't even keep the puréed peas from dribbling out of her mouth just after Mom had spooned them in. I could hardly picture her keeping up during Chutes and Ladders.

"You're lucky to have a new sister."

"Yes, I know," I said, smiling and tilting my head to the right. Mom had also been saying this a lot lately.

When I was escorted out of his office, Mom looked up from a tattered copy of *Psychology Today*. The shrink smiled, and Mom appeared elated and deflated, happy that she didn't mess up her firstborn too badly and sorry that she had wasted the shrink's precious time on a kid who wasn't really the devil's spawn, after all.

When we got out to the car, Mom asked what we did during our hour, which wasn't really an hour but fifty-two minutes and I said so.

"He had me draw a picture of us. Don't worry, I wasn't dumb enough to draw you as monsters."

Shortly after my session, I started kindergarten. Each afternoon, when I stepped off the bus, Mom would meet me at the door and ask, "How was school today?"

"Fine," I'd say in a tiny voice.

"What did you do today?" she'd ask, the space between her eyebrows twitching.

"Nothing."

"Who did you play with at recess?" she'd inquire. At this point, she'd begin kneading her hands.

"No one," I'd say, my voice shaky.

These sorts of responses earned me my favorite dinner, even toys. But the new posture I'd developed—slumped over, eyes down, shoulders up where earmuffs belonged—earned me another trip to the shrink's.

My great aunt Sue rode along and sat with me in the waiting room while Mom was in with him. Delicately and with great pity, Sue asked me how school was going.

I burst into laughter, saying in between giggles, "It's good! I sure pulled a good one on Mom! She thinks I hate it!"

Sue tattled, and Mom confirmed my claim with my teacher, who assured her I was not only enjoying school, but "running it." This was an easy feat. Several of my classmates couldn't read, and two-thirds of them raised their left hands when the teacher asked to see their right. They ate Elmer's glue and sat in awe of the PBS series we watched during milk break, their mouths gaping, their eyes dull like the plastic ones in the fish Papa had mounted in his den.

I didn't care for the TV shows and instead occupied myself by counting the tiles on the lunchroom ceiling and floor, by watching my teacher pull up her socks every time a kid asked her a question she didn't want to answer. Sometimes I timed myself on how long I could stare at the Smith twins' perpetually snotty noses before turning away. Other times I drew on my desk and in my books, anything so I wouldn't think of my sister at home with Mom all to herself.

Did Mom sing to Natalie? Did she tell her she loved her best? More than anything, I feared the day Natalie became old enough to play with my toys while I was away. I imagined Mom conspiring against me, telling her to have a ball but to remember to put them back exactly where I'd left them, as I was "funny" about things being moved out of their place. Eventually, though, the disturbing thought of Natalie playing with my toys gave way to a new obsession—death—and my behaviors were attributed to my being an unchallenged genius, which suited me just fine.

Playing with the Queen of Barbies

Natalie, age 6

My sister ruined my life. Not directly, in a way that would produce tangible evidence and incite appropriate punishment, but through my Barbies and the pathetic existence she created for them.

Life for Shannon and me revolved around our Barbies. On weekends, we would play from the time we woke up until bedtime, breaking only for meals or to watch our favorite sitcoms, from which we derived many of our "plots." Everywhere we went, we would keep our eyes out for suitable Barbie props or clothing. What for most people was a glove, for example, was to Shannon and me four potential legwarmers and a hat. Our Barbies did not glide through the air when they walked, as I had seen my friends' annoyingly do (the few times I allowed them to play with me); they stayed close to the ground, both literally and figuratively.

Nothing happened to our Barbies that couldn't happen in real life. We even had our own "families," whose personas never changed, no matter how much we—or rather I—disliked them.

Although our parents provided each of us with an extensive Barbie collection, Shannon made it clear to me that *all* of the dolls' futures lay in her hands. If I told Mom or did not cooperate, she warned me, my Barbies would be murdered by "Blackbone"— a serial killer she must have invented just for this purpose—who threatened his future victims by playing ZZ Top's "Sharp-Dressed Man" into their tiny telephones. If Shannon detected any evidence of my straying off her playroom path, she would instantly set me straight by humming the first bar of the dreadful song.

And so it was on that day that Shannon created my family, the Viskers. Wes Visker, a Western Ken with a duct-taped torso (his rubber band broke, causing him never to buck again), was the owner, operator, and sole customer of Wes's Gas, which was housed beneath a dusty end table. At sundown, rather than going home to his family, he would drive his wheel-less Bronco down to the Chug-a-Lug. The Chug-a-Lug, a hubcap on the basement floor, was the bar where everyone—until booze obliterated—knew his name.

Wes's wife, Tracy, a frumpish brunette doll who came boxed with two hideous toddler twins, slaved away her days at the local lard factory. Her boss was Mrs. Houston, the town nut and a rummage sale connoisseur, modeled after Gabby. Mrs. Houston lived in a trailer, which was really the vent in our dining room, and delighted in reminiscing to passersby about the best sale she'd ever attended—"You wouldn't believe it. There were *so* many rackets: ping pong rackets, paddle ball rackets, and even *bat-a-mitten*." People generally avoided Mrs. Houston's trailer, except poor Tracy, when she had to tell her boss she couldn't come in to work because the twins were sick—again. Calling in was not an option, as neither Tracy nor Mrs. Houston had a phone.

When the twins were well, Tracy was forced to leave them with her 19-year-old daughter, Elizabeth. Despite her age, Elizabeth was a Skipper doll, and I desperately tried to make her taller by cramming her flat feet into the tops of cast-off Western Barbie boots. Shannon was quick to inform me that this looked "stupid," so I didn't even attempt to enhance Elizabeth's flat chest. Elizabeth spent her babysitting hours making out with whichever boy was desperate enough to have her that day. Tracy's other option was to leave the kids with the pre-teen Kate, also a Skipper, a tomboyish bully who frequently resided at the juvenile detention center. Kate's partner in crime was Curly—not a Barbie at all, but a four-inch, bigheaded Strawberry Shortcake doll—who lived in a decrepit upper (a drawer) in the inner city (the kitchen).

Surprisingly, the Viskers lived in a Barbie Dream House. Its elevator, however, had mysteriously disappeared. The only explanation I can think of now is that Santa must have posed too great a threat to Shannon's omnipotence. And to her discontent, because we shared a playroom, the Viskers had to live in the suburbs, just feet away from Shannon's rich, talented, and beautiful Bordeaux family. This family was like no family I knew. They sat together at dinner, asked permission to be excused, and said "blessifyou" if one of them sneezed. I didn't know the definition of "blessifyou," but it sounded very impressive in Shannon's British accent.

Ken Bordeaux, a Malibu Ken, was a handsome and well-respected real estate tycoon. His wife, Rachel, a Malibu Barbie, was a successful fashion designer/model/entrepreneur. Her famous boutique, with its pink and blue display cases, long satin gloves, and fancy hats tilted on stands, had once been one of my Christmas presents. Ken and Rachel's children more than lived up to their parents' expectations. The popular teenaged Stephanie was an Olympic gold-medal-winning gymnast. LaVonne, Kate's age, was a genius world chess champion (and not the nerdy variety). And Nan, their youngest, was a cute little blonde who charmingly bossed around her nanny.

Because Shannon's Dream House was only a fragment of what she dreamed, she extended her estate across two full walls, using boxes she brilliantly decorated with wallpaper samples and magazine cutouts. The remaining space, that which wasn't corrupted by my three-foot eyesore, was used for a swimming pool, by which Rachel maintained her tan lines, and a field in which her golden, shiny-maned horses could run free. My single three-legged horse lived in my yard and kitchen.

Despite their proximity, the Viskers and Bordeaux remained strictly acquaintances, though the Bordeaux didn't acknowledge my family at all when one of their famous friends visited (e.g.,

Michael Jackson one Christmas day). The Bordeaux children were forbidden to associate with mine, beyond a "How do you do?" The Viskers couldn't reply anyway, because they didn't know what the inquiry meant. Occasionally, however, LaVonne and Kate would sneak off to create some mischief, such as when they went to the zoo, broke into the reptile cage, and let loose poisonous snakes (gummy worms). Although LaVonne was always the mastermind behind these schemes, when their parents found out, Kate was always to blame. Despite the known consequences for Kate, these were the moments I lived for, when Kate and LaVonne put their differences aside and simply enjoyed each other's company. I must have enjoyed Shannon's company, too, because I rarely questioned the unfairness of it all—or perhaps I was just trying to save my Barbies' limbs and hair. In any case, if I wanted the game to continue, I would have to play it her way. I've been playing it ever since.

Apples to Oranges

Shannon, age 9

When I grew up, I wanted to be famous— a beautiful peasant-turned-royal or international box-office smash, though I'd settle for being the envy-inducing wife of a frenzy-inducing British pop star. Natalie wanted to be a man who sold apples.

"You want to be a man who sells apples?" Mom asked in the chipper voice everyone used when talking to Natalie.

"Yep, by the side of the road."

I rolled my eyes, checking my reflection in the picture window while doing so. There was no way my sister would become famous doing *that*.

Mom did not look alarmed by Natalie's aspirations. "Why do you want to be a man who sells apples, honey?"

"It would be fun," she said, as if this were obvious. "Or I'd like to have lots of dogs. And really, really long hair so I don't have to wear underwear."

There was a good chance my sister would have been content with a life of apple peddling and poop scooping. For whatever reason, she lacked my insatiable appetite for being best, first, most, and only. This deficiency displayed itself in behaviors I found unfathomable, such as sharing and letting others win.

Each Easter, after following a trail of activity books, stuffed bunnies, and new tennis shoes, we'd find our grand prizes: near laundry hamper-sized baskets brimming with candy and Barbies. I used this to make my less-fortunate classmates jealous, "accidentally" spilling my bounty from my desk when the classroom grew quiet. Natalie actually shared her jellybeans and even her coveted Bumpy Jumpy popcorn bunny, and within days, her basket held nothing but sparse patches of plastic grass.

"Gimme some lick," I'd say, barging in to Natalie's bedroom to demand licorice. She'd be coloring or playing teacher to a bed full of stuffed animals, her trove sitting out in the open.

"I'm saving it for Lori," she said. Lori had been her best friend since she was three, which meant anything either of them owned was communal property.

"I said gimme some lick!"

Natalie hurled herself onto her basket as if dampening a fire. By this time she was not quite the pushover she once was. She'd also developed quite the shrill scream, and since Mom was right in the next room, pillaging was out of the question. I had to pull out the big guns: the poor little puppy.

I wrinkled my forehead, frowned, made my wrists go limp, and held my hands up under my chin. "Naddowie," I said in my cutest voice, "I'm a poor widdo puppy, and nobody wuvs me. I just want some wicowice."

"Shannon, don't!'" she screamed, clutching her basket's pink, braided handle.

"Pwease give me some wicowice. I'm so hungwy and nobody feeds me," I said, whimpering and weakly barking as I hobbled toward her, dragging my left leg behind me. Her grip loosened as I morphed from cunning manipulator to gimpy, hungry mutt.

I made off with all of her licorice and half of her other loot.

Winning over Natalie was somewhat easier than swiping her candy, because she thought it fun to simply play games for the sake of playing. If it was more important for a classmate to win, she'd let him, tripping in the last leg during foot races or bungling an easy setup in Chinese checkers. However, there was no way she could throw the 1983 Channel 9 Christmas Coloring Contest, and Natalie and I won the 4-to-6 and 8-to-10 categories, respectively. Our drawings were shown on each prime-time commercial break, and we became celebrities at the gas station and Ben Franklin.

Although our newfound fame gave me the perfect excuse to strut about town like a television pimp, it had the opposite effect on Natalie, who never appreciated her legions of admirers. From the time she was a toddler, attention for her big brown eyes and full red lips caused Natalie to stash her head between Mom's legs or to hole up behind whatever store display was nearest.

"Mom, make them stop looking at me," she'd whine whenever someone's adoring gaze found her—which it always did.

"It's okay, Natalie. Smile, they think you're pretty," Mom would reassure her, patting my sister's wavy, waist-length hair.

"No, make them stop looking at me!" she'd repeat, scampering for safety. When this caused even more attention—as well as a generous sprinkling of "oohs," "aahs," and "isn't she darling"s— she would resort to glaring at her fans. Though I'd never admit it, Natalie's glare scared even me. Once, when peering out from behind a pyramid of Campbell's soup cans, she locked in on an elderly lady, whose smile quickly collapsed into a frown. As the woman turned her cart around and shuffled away without her can of tomato paste, she commented to Mom that if looks could kill, she'd surely be dead.

Natalie's discomfort did not dissipate at home and was especially apparent when the winning entries would flash across the screen.

"My God, your category had no competition at all! Look at the third-place effort!" I'd say, gloating over the lopsided manger scene some Kevin kid from a neighboring town had drawn. Baby Jesus resembled a corncob resting in Mary's stumpy arms.

"He can't help it if he can't draw good," Natalie muttered, no doubt fantasizing about pinning her blue ribbon onto little Kevin's chest.

Eventually Natalie began getting up during commercial

breaks, probably ashamed of having burst the bubbles of the less artistic Channel 9 viewers.

It was around this time that I realized I could use my sister's kindness: her slightly down-turned chocolate-colored eyes, her demure smile, her ever-pleasant attitude. They were the makings of a fine sidekick, one who inspired trust and didn't want a cut of the glory.

The Candy Man Can't

Natalie, age 6

By the time I was five, I was allergic to all of the finest ingredients known to man—Yellow 5, Blue 1, and my favorite, FD&C Red 40. Even the smallest drop of artificial food coloring would cause my eyes to water and my nose to run faster than I could get to the center of a Tootsie Pop. Then there was the sneezing, the most attention-grabbing and, hence, horrific part. These were not the cute little "hat-choo"s of other girls my age. My sneezes were more like volcanic eruptions. When it happened in class and everyone would turn to catch me tangled in a web of facial fluids, I would either have to discreetly wipe the snot, spit, and tears on my clothes or, worse, walk up to the teacher's desk and grab a Kleenex or ask to use the bathroom. (Even when I simply had to pee, I would hold it for hours rather than approach her with the dreaded question.) To make things worse, I couldn't ask

Mom for tissues to keep in my desk unless I was sick; any other time she would know I'd given in to the playground candy pushers.

As if being deprived of artificial food coloring was not bad enough, chocolate was soon added to the list of foods I was denied. This caused a somewhat less conspicuous symptom—hives on my forearms. At least I could hide them with long sleeves, and despite making me smell like a diaper, Desitin usually kept the itching to a minimum. So Mom had to revise her annual note to my teacher: "Natalie is allergic to artificial food coloring <u>and</u> chocolate. Please do not allow her to have anything that contains or might contain these things." That left two candies that I could eat: "vanilla" taffy, which looked and tasted like dried glue, and Bit-o-Honey, which I figured came in bits because a larger portion would be too unbearable. Because no one in her right mind would consider these products treats, whenever someone in my class had a birthday, he or she passed around things like chocolate cupcakes or Dreamsicles. To prevent me from feeling left out, the teacher would send me to the cafeteria to pick up my treat: a butter-logged sponge they called "garlic bread." Although the lunch ladies knew my situation—Mom had written them a note too—my fear of approaching them never ceased. At least as terrifying was the trip down the hall, past the seventh and eighth grade rooms and the wisecracking janitor, Larry, who, between verses of "Wild Thing," teased me about smuggling bread from the kitchen. If I was lucky, the teacher would allow Lori to go with me, and we'd make the journey more fun and less scary by skipping and holding hands. The handholding was a risk in itself, because if Shannon happened to see us, she would point, snicker, and call us "lesbos." When I returned to class, I would politely nibble on the crust—the only part that wasn't soggy—while the other kids obnoxiously slurped their popsicles or smacked their frosting-caked lips.

Milk break, too, was problematic, as I was also lactose intolerant. I was convinced this afternoon event was designed specifically to make me feel like even more of an outcast. I was allowed to eat the crackers gooped with peanut butter out of giant tubs, but to wash them down, I had to drink the Mom-forbidden fountain water laced with other kids' drool. I didn't like milk anyway, but I did like the idea of having my very own little carton, and I longed to sniff the mingling aromas of cardboard and souring dairy.

The greatest problem, however, was Halloween, when the trick was finding a treat I could actually consume. Mom would drive Shannon and me down our road and the dirt roads forking off it, as there was no sidewalk and an average of a half-mile between each house. I would follow Shannon up to the houses, mumbling "trick or treat," or sometimes just moving my lips to her words. As I watched the rainbows of candy streaming into my bag, I'd smile and mutter "thank you," though I really felt like crying. A few of our kind neighbors who knew about my allergies set aside a special treat for me—an apple or a few pennies—which they would proudly plop into my bag, believing they were really doing me a favor.

When we got home, Shannon and I would dump our bags out on the living room floor. After plucking out a few Bit-o-Honeys, or if I was really lucky, a popcorn ball, and giving them to me, Shannon would scoop up the rest in one big sweep and proceed to eat it in front of me.

Despite having to give up almost all of my candy, Halloween was nonetheless one of my favorite holidays. I still got to dress up, my most memorable costume being the one Mom made when I was in kindergarten—a mouse. Although the clip-on nose caused my eyes to water (I may as well have just eaten the candy), I was impressed by the trap she cleverly attached to my tail. And I felt warm and safe in the big furry suit, its only opening a small hole for my painted face.

Trying on the costume at home, I got sick to my stomach worrying that the other kids would think it was dumb and wishing I was tiny enough to slide through a crack if they did. Once I got to school, however, I felt wonderful. Parading around the room with Raggedy Ann and a slew of witches and princesses, I strangely felt I belonged. The judges did not choose my costume as the best, which was fine. I had no desire to be singled out, and I knew in my heart that, had there been a category for mice, surely I would have won.

Of Cocoa and Womanhood

Shannon, age 9

THOUGH SHE WAS ALWAYS EXPECTING TRAGEDY
where Natalie and I were concerned, the real thing never failed to
catch Mom off guard.

My stomach was churning, my head throbbing. We had just
one bathroom and Natalie wasn't vacating it. The only modest
member of our household, she had the door locked, forcing me to
rifle through the junk drawer for Bic pen innards to pop the lock.

"Natalie, I mean it. I have to go now!" I was about to pick the
lock when she exited, cowering in anticipation of my wrath. I
pushed past her without incident, too sick to argue.

When I pulled down my pants, I saw that my white cotton
underwear was covered in blood. I screamed for Mom, who ran to
me like a puppy to a teat.

"I'm bleeding," I pronounced solemnly, already picturing my

funeral. White flowers filled the room, and all of the women wore tiny black hats with netting that covered their tear-streaked faces. My classmates sobbed uncontrollably, wondering who would become their new leader, who would remind them where they fit in without me there to tell them. All of the teachers shared what they had learned from me, a student with wisdom well beyond her years—truly the most advanced and attractive third grader Tripoli Elementary had ever seen the likes of. A flag folded into a neat triangle would be placed on Mom's lap as tears streamed down her face. Reporters broadcasting live from the funeral home would let the images speak for themselves, as they'd be too choked up to form words. "Only the good die young," people would murmur.

"Did you hear me? Is it coming from your butt or from the front?" Mom shrieked.

"I don't know. There's a lot of blood."

"Just sit here. Don't move!"

Mom ran into the kitchen and picked up the phone. "Keep talking to me," she yelled to me as she dialed and then barked at my father, "Kerry, turn that damn television down!"

"What are you jawing about?" he asked, clearly inconvenienced that his daughter's hemorrhaging had interrupted the Yanks in the bottom of the seventh.

"She's bleeding! I don't know where it's coming from! I'm calling the clinic right now! You're going to have to drive!" Then she whispered, "She's losing a lot of blood, so we'll have to be fast." It had been a few months since one of us girls had been rushed in for emergency medical care, the last trip being for Natalie, who sucked a bead up her nose while making candy cane Christmas tree ornaments. I was secretly jealous each time it was my sister, rather than I, in a doctor's care. By now, it was not the nurse's attention I craved, but the drama of their workplace. It had been years now that I'd been praying for mono, as I enjoyed watching the shiny needle plunging into my arm when getting a blood test. Now what I coveted was an IV with which I could dance, like Gene Kelly with a lamppost.

My father didn't reply, which indicated the commercial break had ended. He was as lax about bodily injuries and sickness as Mom was hyper-vigilant. His self-treated logging injuries were the stuff holiday entertainment was made of—a right ring finger that could bend sideways at a 90-degree angle, a sawed kneecap, tales of being pinned under a maple tree as his lungs filled with blood.

Mom was apparently on hold, and after some time, Dad asked, "Did you explain to her what's happening so she's not scared?"

"What do you mean explain what's happening! I don't know what's wrong with her!"

"She's got her damn period, that's what's wrong with her," he said, readjusting the volume.

And so I became a woman.

One can't blame Mom for not guessing that puberty was the culprit. I was only 9 years old. And I was always moody, so no hormonal changes were evident. There were signs, however.

Earlier that year, I had sprouted breasts. Not those of the Raisinet-sized, training-bra-optional variety, either. They were B-cup woman breasts that bounced uncontrollably when I played kickball or double-dutch on the playground. This greatly pleased Gabby, who took to beaming at them and pointing out their finer attributes to Uncle Jeff and his teenaged friends. "Oooh, just look at how full her bosom is, oooh, and so high," she'd say over lemonade, or "Shannon, show your uncle how voluptuous you are. Bridget Bardot, you look voluptuous like Bridget Bardot!" (Gabby pronounced voluptuous "volumptuous.")

Then an even greater horror had descended upon my body: pubic hair. And just days before Girl Scout camp! As the other members of my troop packed their teddy bears and Holly Hobby sleeping bags, I stood in the bathroom, dry-shaving with my dad's razor. At camp, my fellow Scouts sat around the campfire telling ghost stories and giggling about boys. I inconspicuously scratched my stubble and feared whatever other physical changes might be in store. Making excuses about why I changed my clothes in the outhouse should have earned me a merit badge.

Grown men began leering at me, and sixth grade boys called me Swiss Miss, as though puberty and cocoa went hand-in-hand. Meanwhile, Natalie was blissfully young. At five, the only curves she sported were her knees. I tried to play with her and the neighborhood kids, but playing castle—which I usually adored, since the other children were my servants or admiring charges from my kingdom—seemed foolish. Riding my bike was uncomfortable, as the pad I was forced to wear was approximately the same length and width of my banana seat. Pretending that we were going on dates with our imaginary boyfriends took on a tawdry feel; after all, I knew from a particularly gripping ABC After School Special titled "I think I'm Having a Baby" what my period meant. Armed with a historical romance novel and a condom wrapper, it was I who had taught every kid on County Road D about the birds and the bees and pirates with throbbing manhoods.

I had no choice: I stopped skipping, gave up Nancy Drew, and boxed up my toys. Folding my arms across my chest, I walked uncertainly into the space between girl and woman.

Uncommon Scents

Natalie, age 6

"Dad? Dad. Dad. Dad! Daaaaaad!!!" No matter how loud or long I said it, the response was always the same: silence. After an exhausting day of work in the woods, Dad would kick off his boots in a scatter of sawdust and plop into his broken La-Z-Boy. There he would sit for hours, staring absently and picking his teeth with a twig plucked from the dying plant beside his chair.

Though most of Dad's time at home was spent in front of the TV, in the winter, he had the responsibility of splitting logs for firewood and fueling the stove. The wood stove was in the basement, my favorite place in the house. Dimly lit and quiet, the downstairs was nothing like the upstairs—no glaring lights or blaring TV, like those that stayed on around the clock in every room despite Dad's monthly lectures about "subsidizing the electric company" and his dramatic demonstrations of how to operate various switches. There was none of Mom's too-loud telephone chatter or incessant clicking on her typewriter. Most importantly, the basement was a place Shannon rarely ventured, except by accident—like the time her Barbies' canary-yellow convertible took a wrong turn and wound up at The Chug-a-Lug. (Oh, how Rachel screamed when she stepped into the hubcap to ask for directions and got dust on her white suit.)

The basement was rarely cleaned, but when it was, Dad and I were the only ones who would do it. At least once a year, Dad would sort out everything from tools to spare change and neatly stack his wood along one wall. Sometimes I would help him, and he'd praise me for sharing his close attention to detail. When the organizing was done, we would thoroughly sweep the cracked cement floor. He even let me push around the giant broom, kicking up clouds of dust that made my face look as sooty as his often did. Like Dad, I didn't mind the dirt.

I enjoyed these special occasions, but even on an average day, the basement was fun. So every time I heard the creak of the stove's door and the thud of wood, I tiptoed down the steps.

I would stand by patiently until Dad was done feeding the stove and wait for his invitation. "Hey, Nat, come 'ere," he'd say, waving me over to the wood pile, which, in its normal state, was a lopsided mound created by hurling logs through a dislodged window. Dad would then display his vast knowledge of wood by asking me to select a piece and hold it in front of his nose. With his sun-creased eyelids closed tightly, he would identify it—correctly every time—as ash, cherry, or maple. Then it was my turn. I usually guessed wrong, but Dad didn't care. He would calmly describe the characteristics of each scent and tell me to try again. Although wood wafting seemed to me a useless skill, I wanted to master it, simply to make him proud. At the same time, part of me wanted to fail, so I could hear his descriptions again. Whether it was the lull of his voice or simply that he was talking to me, I never tired of hearing them.

The best times, however, were when Dad would pluck at his guitar. Tottering on a log, he would rock back and forth, bowing his head and shaking it, then lifting it and nodding to the ceiling. Sometimes I would spin myself dizzy around the steel posts. Other times I would prop my own log beside him and make up accompanying lyrics. My favorite song was "Seemio": "Once there was a frog/on a sunny day/he fell off a swing and broke his leg/and then he couldn't play. [Chorus] Seemio, oh, Seemio. Seemio, oh, Seemio. Seemio. Seemio. See-mi-o." Dad quickly learned the words, and even began to sing along, adding verses of his own. He stuck with my unfortunate frog theme and never questioned the absurdity of an amphibian on a swing or roller skates, as Shannon surely would have done.

Dad and I didn't relate to each other often, but when we did, we related well. We had a lot more in common than the darkness of our hair. Though we didn't see it at the time, we had a lot in common with Seemio, too. Although Dad was tough when it came to physical injuries—like when he sawed his knee open with his chainsaw and wanted to go back to work the next day—he wasn't so tough when it came to other people. Because he was so "good natured," "laid back," and "easy going," it seemed that everyone, from his family to his wood buyers, was always taking advantage of him. When they did, he wouldn't stand up for himself. Mom, who could be assertive with anyone, didn't seem to understand this.

"What do you mean he's not paying you until next week? We need groceries in the house!"

Dad would look down and shake his head. "I just didn't have the heart to ask."

"Oh, Kerry," Mom would say, "Why do you have to act like such a victim?"

I supposed I was a victim too because I let Shannon, and peoples' opinions of me, dictate my every move. Like Dad and Seemio, when I was knocked down, I didn't brush myself off and get back in the game; I would sit on the sidelines and pout.

Looking back now, I see that perhaps more significant than Seemio's misfortunes was his name: See-me-oh. In a family in which our outspoken, light-haired opposites—Shannon and Mom—literally *took* center stage, our cry to be seen seems fitting. Or maybe it wasn't a cry but a celebration: Because in our house's dark underbelly, Dad and I were—if only by each other—finally, gloriously seen.

Nylon Is Thicker than Water

Shannon, age 11

Everyone who was anyone wore them.
Boy George, the punks I'd seen on MTV, both of the Coreys. Being a someone, I needed to have them: parachute pants.

"What are parachute pants?" Mom asked in response to my begging.

"Duh. They're, like, only the coolest thing."

"Like the legwarmers you had to have and then wore for ten minutes?"

"No. Way cooler."

"Like the jelly shoes you loved but now refuse to wear?"

"You know I can't wear them now that Dawn Kittelson has them!"

"Like the boxing shoes you can't even find now?"

"This is different. If I don't get them . . . I'll *die*."

"Oh, well, then, I'd better get right on it. God knows I'd have to get you something *really* special to wear to your funeral."

For weeks, I scoured clothing stores and found only Lee jeans, John Deere hats, and overpriced T-shirts reading, "My parents went to Minocqua and all they brought me was this stupid T-shirt."

"They're made out of nylon," I'd say to clueless shopkeepers wearing floral print dresses or worse.

"Periscope pants, you say?"

"No, parachute pants. You know, with zippers all over them? Billy Idol wears them."

"Billy who?"

I hadn't been so enthralled with a material object since first grade. Consumed with desire for white roller skates with pink wheels, I tried to earn money for them by putting price tags on objects—Dad's baseball trophies ($1 for the lot), our record player ($1.50), Mom's winter coat (75 cents)—and carting them to the edge of our gravel driveway. Unfortunately, the only people who drove on our road were en route to Floyd's Auto Salvage, and they weren't in the market for Natalie's Grumpy Care Bear.

My daydreams shifted from receiving standing ovations for some feat or another to walking in London with my punk friends, our parachute pants swishing between our thighs, our adjoined nose rings jangling in the wind.

And then I found them. At K-mart, in men's clearance, tucked behind a Fruit of the Loom display. I snatched the only small amidst a sea of XXLs and raced to find Mom. She and Natalie were in the toothpaste aisle.

"Mom, Mom, look! I found them! My parachute pants!" I caressed the tiny square pattern stitched into the flimsy, black fabric. At long last, my harrowing journey had ended. I'd found my Holy Grail, and it was just $4.

"Can I get parachute pants?" Natalie asked sweetly.

"How much are they?" Mom asked.

"Four dollars! Can you believe it? They're worth, like, a hundred!"

"I want parachute pants," Natalie squealed.

"They don't have them in your size," I said, a bit too gleefully. The previous year, I began losing my molars and kept them in a small plastic box given to me by my dentist. Because she hadn't yet lost her teeth, Natalie saved her chicken pox scabs in the top drawer of her dresser.

"Okay, you can get them, but put the magazine back," Mom said.

"But I want parachute pants!" Natalie pleaded, her bottom lip shaking like Gabby's hand when she wrote a check.

"Too bad, you can't have them!" I said, clutching my find to my chest and inhaling the faintly plastic smell. Natalie started whimpering.

"Natalie, how about we get you a headband? You'd like a headband, wouldn't you?" Mom offered.

Natalie started bawling, and then, in a truly Shannon-worthy *coup de théâtre,* began choking. This, she'd learned after downing half a tub of Vaseline recently, would *really* get Mom's attention. And for the first time in her life, my sister didn't seem to care if it would attract the attention of others.

When her spewing first began, shoppers scurried to our aisle, expecting to find a blue light special. Mom looked horrified, as if she was actually reconsidering her decision to not be a pig parent. She threw out gift suggestions to appease her—dolls, a dress, even candy—and I just stared at Natalie in awe. She rasped, gagged, and flailed herself about in a stunning display of showmanship. She screamed that she hated me, that she hated Mom, and that she hated K-mart. She even screamed that she hated parachute pants.

Natalie's resentment did not end when we got to the car, or even when we got home. In fact, it lasted well into the '90s, coming out of dormancy every time she felt slighted. It became a running joke everyone but my sister found funny: "Yes, and Shannon got parachute pants," Mom would say with a roll of her eyes if Natalie complained that I got to go somewhere and she didn't.

I only wore them for about a week, but in my sister's head, I always wore the pants.

The Gift Graph

Natalie, age 8

For our family, Christmas has always been a time of revelation. Love that seemed latent throughout the rest of the year became evident through the care Dad took in selecting and cutting a tree (albeit off of a neighbor's property) and the patience Mom miraculously mustered to decorate dozens of cookies and make ornaments with us girls. And despite any economic hardship, our parents always made sure there was an overabundance of presents under the tree. Although Shannon and I appreciate all of this now, when we were children, Christmas revealed only one thing: who was the favored child.

Each Christmas morning, sometimes before sunrise, Shannon and I would jump on Mom and Dad's bed, bellowing, "Time to open presents!" As they grudgingly untangled themselves from their covers and tugged on their clothes, we would scamper to the tree and begin our ritual. After drawing circles on Mom's typing paper to note how the radius of packages around the tree compared to previous years, we would carefully but quickly divide our presents. We did not shake them like other children did. To us, it was not so important what was in the packages; all that mattered was who had more. Once Mom and Dad entered the room, the paper began flying, and before they could rub the crust from their eyes, we were hidden behind our respective mounds, discreetly beginning our counts. When we emerged, and Mom and Dad were opening their presents to each other, we could finally eye up each other's goods and exchange totals.

One year, after two consecutive years of coming up short, I decided to draw a graph to document the injustice and state my case to Mom and Dad. A line in red Crayon represented Shannon's gift history, while a line in blue represented mine. Red peaks, like the rooftops of the castles Shannon insisted she would someday inhabit, towered across the graph, the last reaching the top of the page. Beneath a massive gap of white were tiny blue bumps, which flatlined halfway across the page. I don't recall Mom and Dad's exact responses to my presentation, but the words "greedy" and "ungrateful," and Shannon's snickering in the background, come to mind.

I grew to expect the unfairness from Mom and Dad. Year round, Shannon got more, like the parachute pants I had convinced myself I wanted, the catalyst of fights for years to come. I don't think I asked for much, candy at the grocery store or a new notebook, while Shannon demanded each new trend before anyone else in school had the chance to get it.

What I could not understand, however, was Santa's unfairness. After all, he knew who was naughty and who was nice. He was the only one, besides me and God, who was witness to Shannon's bullying. So why wasn't he punishing her? The day my question was answered, Shannon and I were sitting in the living room with Mom, discussing what we'd like from Santa that year.

Out of the blue, or the red and green, Shannon blurted out, "You know who Santa is, don't you, Natalie?" It seemed like a very silly question. *Santa is Santa. Just like Mom is Mom and you—unfortunately—are you.* But Shannon's snotty tone, and the glare Mom flashed her across the room, told me something was not right. A sense of ill-being suddenly came over me, like on the nights I would lie in my pitch-black room and ask myself, *Who are you and why are you here?* Shannon must have read my confused and disturbed look and decided to help me out. "Well, she's wearing glasses, a flannel shirt . . ." I looked over at Mom: her eyes were bulging and her half smile was not so happy. At that moment, it was as if my Christmas spirit was a fragile ornament that Shannon had shaken off of the tree. I would never put the shards back together; I could, however, get even.

A week before Christmas, figuring my holiday was already ruined, I sneaked into Mom and Dad's closet to begin the gift count early. The next day, as Shannon and I were waiting for Mom at the drugstore, I began to sing, "I know what you're getting for

Christmas. I know what you're getting for Christmas."

"No, you don't," Shannon said coolly, chomping her gum.

"You're getting a Swatch watch, Guess jeans, Nike Airs . . ."

She jerked her head at me. "What are you doing? Shut up."

"A new boom box, an Oxford sweatshirt, some stupid little—"

"Shut up!" Mom was coming, so Shannon couldn't wring my neck. She just covered her ears, screaming, as I continued down the list.

I was grounded that Christmas, and my gift graph plummeted. This time, I didn't care.

Family Jewels

Shannon, age 12

"**All right, untie your shoe.** No, your left one. And we've got to mess up your hair a bit more." I thrust Natalie's head forward and began batting at her mass of hair as if it were under attack by killer bees.

"Ouch, you're hurting me," she whimpered, trying to straighten up and brush her hair out of her eyes. My sister was only 8 but had Grandma Kring's long, elegant fingers. I had Dad's thick knuckles.

I stepped back to assess my creation.

"No, that's too much. I'm going for tired and slightly pathetic, not trailer trash. We don't want these people to think we're from around here." I raked my fingers through a snarl at the crown of Natalie's head, and she yelped.

"Okay, good. Do you have your lines down?"

"Why don't we just go back and watch TV," Natalie proposed. "C'mon, it'll be fun."

"But what if Mom finds out?" This was one of the first times that Mom had let us stay at Gabby's while she ran to the grocery store. She had said we could play outside as long as we stayed away from the garage, which contained an arsenal of metal objects that could cause tetanus. I interpreted her loosely to mean that we could go anywhere rusty nails were not.

"Mom won't find out. Gabby's too busy exercising to notice we're gone." Gabby had recently purchased a secondhand exercise bike, which she had positioned in front of her velvet Elvis tapestry in her Pepto-Bismol-colored laundry room.

"But I don't want to!"

"Tough titty said the kitty, but the milk tastes good," I mimicked Gabby. Natalie's eyes started reddening, so I tried a smile on her. "Hey, it'll just be one house. I promise."

Natalie turned and looked over her shoulder, as if she was considering fleeing. I grabbed her wrist.

"Shannon, don't!" she screamed.

"Look here, you little bitch! If you don't come with me right now, I'll tell Mom that you watched Gabby's lady prison movie with her last night after she went to bed." After a fight with Dad the previous night, Mom, Natalie, and I had spent the night at Gabby's because Uncle Jerry already had guests.

"Okay, I guess. But let's hurry."

I had never taken my sister along on any of my adventures, as she didn't share my penchant for lying and, in fact, felt it her moral obligation to bust me in my fantastical tales. She was still nursing the wounds I had inflicted two days prior, when she'd interrupted me as I explained to a cute bagger at Nelson's Grocery how I—an only child from London—came to live in the Northwoods of Wisconsin. It was a story I'd been telling for a long time and was born of my love for the NBC sitcom *The Facts of Life* and Duran Duran. In it, I told of life "back home"—of being the most popular student at a posh London boarding school. I would sneak out of my dorm window at night and travel to Birmingham—on foot or on one of those scooters like Audrey Hepburn's in *Roman Holiday*—to watch my older, wiser, and even more popular boyfriend Nick Rhodes of Duran Duran. Nick dedicated his weekdays to pining after me, while his weekends were spent playing keyboards in clubs packed with screaming, writhing girls who wanted a piece of my man. At this point of the story, I whispered in what I was sure was a perfect English accent that my blatantly lower middle-class parents and sister, dreadfully unfashionable, were the only distant, distant, *distant* relatives the executors of my real parents' estate could locate after their untimely death involving a cream-colored convertible and a countryside game of croquet.

"All right, look as pathetic as you can," I instructed Natalie. "Shouldn't be too hard for you."

"How's this?" Natalie asked reluctantly, peering out from behind her tangled bangs.

"Perfect. Let's start that way and work down to the end of the street, then come back and hit the other side," I said, gesturing to the small houses across the street from my grandparents' new house. They'd recently moved into town, into a clean, working-class neighborhood where each house had more lawn ornaments than the next.

We cut across the neighbor's balding yard, weaving in and out of the maze of kitsch: spray-painted wicker baskets filled with faded silk flowers, wooden one-dimensional cutouts of the backsides of gardeners, and even though it was the 1980s, swollen-lipped black boys fishing or holding lanterns.

The doorbell hung on a frayed cord like an eyeball dislodged from its socket. I knocked on the dented screen door until the blare of *The Price is Right* went quiet and a woman with heavy, pendulous breasts peered through the screen.

"Excuse me, ma'am," I said with a smile. "My sister and I are sorry to disturb you, but my aunt, she's visiting from Seattle. She lost her engagement ring somewhere on this road when she was on her walk early this morning and we're trying to find it for her. You haven't by any chance seen a diamond ring, have you? You can't miss it. It's big as a quarter and just as shiny. My aunt, she's all hoity toity, and it was her favorite ring." "Hoity toity" was a term Gabby used to describe her sister Mary.

The woman crossed her arms over her chest and glanced back at her TV, saying impatiently, "Nah, I didn't see a ring. My soap's about to start."

"Well, thanks. We'd appreciate it if you keep your eyes open."
I turned to Natalie, and in a stage whisper added, "Let's keep looking. We want to find the ring and get the $500 reward before
anyone else does!"

Natalie missed her cue. Instead, she stared straight ahead,
tugging nervously on her bottom lip.

"We want to find the ring and get the reward, *right, Natalie?*" I
repeated. When she didn't respond, I slowly put my arm around
her and pinched her back as hard as I could.

"Yes, let's hurry," Natalie said, sounding more like a zombie
than someone embarking on a treasure hunt. I glared at her, waiting for her to do as she was instructed. She turned around and
began running toward the next house, as planned. I followed her.

I glanced back at the lady, whose eyes lit up as she scanned
the large painted rocks lining her driveway.

By the time we reached the end of the street, the ring was the
size of a yo-yo, the reward was $2,500, and half the town was scav-
enging alongside the road, huddling excitedly over pull rings from
soda cans, fish hooks, anything that glittered. Natalie loosened up
a bit, though she begged to go home when I suggested that the
reluctant cripple on the corner get in the game, pushing him over
the edge with, "With that motorized scooter of yours, you'll have
a clear advantage over those who have to use their legs to work
their way down Leather Avenue."

"What the hell is going on out there?" Mom asked when she
came back from shopping. Natalie and I had just returned to

Gabby's. "There are people with metal detectors walking the streets, old ladies fishing in the gutters with their bare hands."

I looked at Natalie, waiting to see if she'd tattle. She just smiled, and if I didn't know better, I'd think I saw a sparkle in her eye.

The following weekend, I talked Natalie into joining me once again, and this time, she was less reluctant.

We stood in Gabby's kitchen, filling sandwich bags one-third full with all-purpose flour.

"What are you girls doing with the flour?" she asked. Natalie giggled and blushed. We still had to work on her nerves.

"We're putting it in sandwich bags and pretending it's cocaine," I said.

"Well, don't spill anything on my floor. Mary's coming." This is why I loved staying at Gabby's on the weekend. She'd catch me fake-sobbing on the phone with a suicide hotline operator—which I did for entertainment from time to time, making up stories about being pregnant and homeless or ugly and unpopular—and only warn me that the call had better not be long distance.

I raided Gabby's makeup bag for black kohl eyeliner and smeared dark circles under my eyes. "How do I look?" I asked.

"You look like a druggie," Natalie affirmed, though the only addicts she'd seen were on episodes of *Hunter*. She'd just finished stashing the filled bags under the mattress in the guest bedroom.

"Let's rock," I said, finishing ratting my bangs with a comb scratched with "Orv."

We went to the backyard, and I took my position in a tree. I nodded to Natalie, who ran to where Mark, the gangly, goody-two-shoes neighbor kid, played basketball with his cousins. She said something to them, and the boys stopped and stared up at me. Mark shook his head, and Natalie gestured nervously with her hands. They all ran over to me.

"She's not on drugs!" Mark said, shaking his flat head.

I dangled from a branch by one leg, singing "The Star-Spangled Banner" off-key. "I'm a bird," I said to him, flapping my wings and swinging erratically from side to side.

"She's going to jump," Natalie said meekly. I flashed my eyes at her, and she cleared her throat and recited her line as we had practiced it: "She's gonna jump!"

"Fly bird, fly away," I said. Remembering that drug addicts on television shook, I began convulsing.

"I don't believe it," said Mark.

"I'll show you," Natalie said, heading toward the house. She sounded like a natural now. "I know where she hides the stuff."

The boys followed Natalie, and I barged into the room a few seconds later. They were wide-eyed as Natalie held the corner of the mattress up, exposing our stash.

"Gimme my cocaine," I said to Natalie, slurring like a drunk. She acted afraid and threw a bag at me.

I poured the contents of the bag onto the dresser and took a $1 bill from my pocket. I rolled it and inhaled sharply through my mouth, instantly feeling as if I'd been kicked in the chest. I fell to the floor and struggled to catch my breath. As my face turned from red to blue, the boys ran from the house screaming.

Natalie handled herself like a veteran prankster that day, even when Mark's father—who, it turned out, was a cop—stormed in and seized enough kilos of flour to bake eight batches of cupcakes. I was almost proud to claim her as my distant, distant, *distant* cousin the next time we went to the grocery store.

Spike and Tike

Natalie, age 8

A neighborhood girl was walking on thin ice. This was not good enough for Shannon. "Jump! Jump! Jump!" she began to chant, cuing her chorus to join in as little Bambi shivered atop the transparent sheet. Bambi and her sister Brianne had just moved into the house next door, and this was their initiation.

Every year, at the first sign of spring, the valley at the bottom of the slope on which our house was perched became a pool of water, slush, and ice. The neighborhood kids (a group that, in our unincorporated town, consisted of the eight children residing on our mile of County Road D) would gather there to enjoy winter's remains. Not surprisingly, our activities were always directed by Shannon, sometimes with the help of me, her reluctant assistant.

In summertime, similar gatherings took place. These usually occurred in the woods surrounding our house. Once we played "hide and seek," which entailed Shannon, me, and a couple of carefully selected kids digging holes, covering them with sticks and leaves, and hiding behind trees to wait for the other team (who thought they were actually seeking) to fall into them. Another time, Shannon thought it would be fun to make "potions." This meant mixing together whatever we could find in the back of Dad's pickup—an old jug of water, wood shavings, and, of course, diesel fuel—and daring someone to drink it. When we added baking soda to the mixture and a drop of the concoction burned a hole through Shannon's canvas Keds, I was glad no one ever took us up on the offer.

More shocking than no one getting hurt was that anyone would continue to play with us. Me, they could have taken or left. But with Shannon, they didn't have a choice. Or maybe they did. Yes, they feared her, but at the same time they admired her. You see, at that time, Shannon was not Shannon, but Spike. She had named herself after her hairdo, which was as sharp and daring as her schemes. Who else would have the guts to call the Miracle Ear 800 number and talk them into sending a representative to her own home (and short-tempered mother)? Who else would throw a pencil at the snotty girl on the bus—and laugh when it momentarily stuck in her forehead? Who would send a sample of Depends undergarments to the biggest boy-bully in school and proudly admit to being the culprit? Rumors spread of her masterful pranks, and she soon became the Pied Piper of the playground. Lured by "Little Red Corvette" blaring from the boom box riding on her shoulder, kids would abandon their slides and swing sets and follow her in a trancelike state as she strutted around their childish props.

Spike was not only admired for her actions, but also for her fashion trailblazing. She was the first in school to wear a black fedora, neon sunglasses indoors, fingerless gloves, pleated newsprint pants splattered with paint, and button-down shirts with tuxedo tails. My one fashion claim to fame was being the second in my school to wear jelly shoes. I was preceded, of course, by Spike.

The kids were proud to call Spike their friend, and I must admit, I was proud to call her my sister. Although I was hardly ever picked on (and, surely, Shannon had something to do with that), I was excruciatingly shy. I would break out in hives and vomit at the thought of going to school. I spoke to no one except Lori, and one of my greatest fears was that the bus would be packed and I would have to sit with someone else on the way to school. Or worse yet, I would have to stand in the aisle, all eyes on me. With Spike by my side, that was impossible. Not because she would have made a seat for me, but because, no matter what, all eyes would be on *her*. And for that I was grateful. Shannon was nothing like Bambi's sister, who fortunately pulled her off the ice that day, but she was my savior all the same.

Cowlicks and Hicks

Shannon, age 12

SONYA MORIN WAS THE ME I NEVER HAD.
She lived in a compound in Dar es Salaam, Tanzania, East Africa, where she had bodyguards, holidays (not to be mistaken for the less-impressive-sounding vacations our family never took) in Hong Kong, and an angelic, ruffle-bedecked little sister who had a *real* British accent from attending a *real* boarding school in England.

In 1985, in what I saw as a cruel twist of fate in her otherwise gilt existence, Sonya was sent to Brantwood, Wisconsin, to stay with her aunt Darcy, a hairdresser.

Darcy knew the latest rage in hairstyles, clothes, and diets. The first time I spent the night, she made pasta and placed it on my plate with shiny, silver tongs. After dinner, she watched *St. Elmo's Fire* with us and called Emilio Estevez a "real babe." Before school, Darcy took me into her hair salon and cut my hair for free. When she finished, it spiked just like hers. She even gave me a jar of blue hair gel so I could re-create the look on my own.

Darcy was cool. Radical. Awesome. But Darcy was Sonya's guardian, and Mom was mine.

My mom was a woman who pecked on her electric typewriter all day and sang in a country-folk band at night. (From snooping around on her desk, I knew what she had been writing: stories and long letters to Uncle Jerry, in which she described a woman chasing her with knives and starving her as a child.) She wore geeky Wrangler jeans, my dad's T-shirts, and a generic version of Dolly Parton's 'do. When Mom made spaghetti, she dished up noodles straight from the pot and plopped them onto my plate with a fork. Once, I talked her into renting *St. Elmo's Fire,* and she didn't even want to know who Emilio Estevez was. She only wanted to know what two 12-year-old girls were doing watching a movie with one raunchy sex scene after another. The only thing Mom lusted after was chocolate. If I would have had my way, Sonya would have never met her. Unfortunately, I didn't have any more control over Mom than I had over my hair.

I stood in the bathroom trying to get my cowlick to stand up like the rest of my hair. Darcy had made it look so easy. Just as I got it into place, the door flew open and whacked me in the shin. My cowlick collapsed back to my head.

"Thanks a lot, Mom! I just got my hair to stand up right and you ruined it! I can't go to school looking like this!"

Mom was wearing her brown leather jacket with fringes that ran down the sleeves and across the back. She took her fogged glasses off and reached for the toilet paper. Mom looked like she always did after she sang. The pouches under her eyes were smeared with mascara. Her hair, lacquered with spray, lay in snarled clumps.

"Hurry up. The bus will be here in five minutes and you haven't even found your coat."

"I'm not wearing a winter coat! No one's wearing a winter coat yet."

"They'll be wearing them today. It's so cold out that I never thought Cug would start."

Cug was our $500 Dodge Horizon. With no muffler and rust-chewed doors, Cug got its name from the first three letters of its wired-on license plate. Determined to prolong its miserable life, Dad cobbled together more than Cug's license plate. Pliers permanently held the radiator hose in place, and the handle of Mom's pink Scalpmaster hairbrush was taped where the turn signal arm should have been. Dad said the only problem with Cug was that Mom needed a little practice to learn to drive a five-speed, but we'd had the car for a year already and she still dumped the clutch whenever she tried to move it.

"Cug? Why are you starting Cug now?"

"I have to go up to the corner store. I'm out of cigarettes." Mom rubbed a wad of toilet paper over her scratched lenses. "I hope I make it. I'm right on empty."

I chased Mom down the hallway. "Mom, wait! You can't go now! Wait until after we leave." Great, all I needed was for Mom to break down. All of the kids would see Cug. Worse yet, the bus driver would probably give Mom a ride to the gas station like he did for Gary Swanson's mom when she had a flat tire. Sonya and all of the other kids would laugh and I'd die. I'd just die.

Mom paused to feel Natalie's forehead. "You look peaked, Natalie. Do you feel okay?"

"Mom, did you hear me?" I pleaded. "Don't leave now! Wait for the bus to come."

Mom knelt down next to Natalie, who was still in her pajamas and panda bear slippers. "Shannon, please. I'm trying to find out if your sister's sick. Natalie, where do you feel sick, honey? Point."

"Mom, did you hear me?"

Mom looked up and snapped, "Didn't I tell you to go find your winter coat?" She began stuffing Natalie's arm into her coat. "I'm bringing her with me." Mom grabbed Natalie's quilt and dashed out the door.

As I ran out to the bus, I could hear Cug chugging in the distance. "Your teeth are clattering," Sonya said when I slid into our seat. I rubbed my bare arms and noticed that everyone, including Sonya, was wearing winter coats.

"I couldn't find my coat," I lied.

We started whispering about Jeff Phillips, who was sitting behind us. We agreed that Jeff would be *almost* cute if he didn't have blackheads in his ears.

"Hey, how about we spend the night at your house this weekend?" Sonya said, upon concluding her enlightening briefing on the immaculate pores of the French boys who attended her school back home.

"Actually, my parents are . . . uh, going away this weekend. They're going on holiday or something, I think," I said, feeling guilty for lying to my best friend. "I have to go stay in town with my grandparents."

The notion of Mom and Dad going on a safari or cruise like Sonya's parents was absurd. Lately, they couldn't go into the kitchen together without breaking into a screaming match. But what could I say? I'd run out of plausible excuses for keeping Sonya out of my reality—visiting family members, sick family members, dead family members. What would she think of me if she saw our simple ranch house, or worse yet, my family? I imagined her home resembling Mr. Drummond's penthouse on the sitcom *Diff'rent Strokes*—lots of marble, paintings in massive gold frames. I pictured her sitting with her flaxen-haired older sister, Melanie, at a twenty-seat dining room table under a massive crystal chandelier. They'd giggle over rose-patterned teacups of hot chocolate and tiny sandwiches presented by maids who called them Miss Sonya and Miss Melanie.

Suddenly, the bus squealed to a stop.

I looked out the windshield, and to my horror, saw Cug on the side of the road. Mom stood behind it, flailing her arms.

I slouched down in the seat and heard the creak of the opening bus door.

"Who's the dork in the Daniel Boone duds?" Jeff asked. Sonya snickered.

I peeked over a kindergartner's head just as Mom was helping Natalie into the front seat. Natalie's face peeked out from her tattered quilt and looked the same putrid color as Cug's fake-leather seats.

Mom would have stayed put and talked to the bus driver had Kathy Clarke not tattled to the whole back of the bus that she was my mother.

Jeff poked me in the shoulder. "That's your mom, Shannon?"

"Go squeeze your blackheads, Jeff," I snapped.

"Hi, Mrs. Kring," Jeff called in the voice he used for grown-ups.

Mom turned around. "Hi," she said. Her smile died when she saw me. "Shannon! Where's your winter coat?" Mom's years of belting out lame lyrics gave her enough projection to rattle the bus windows.

By the time we reached the corner store, Natalie's puke was in the wastepaper basket, and Mom's fringed jacket was on me.

Shortly thereafter, Sonya announced that she had to go back to Africa. I didn't cry until her favorite song, "Spies Like Us" by Paul McCartney, came on the radio. When I turned it up, Natalie said, "You probably don't even like this song. You only listen to this song because Sonya likes it."

Sonya and I continued our friendship for years, via messages passed through Darcy and brightly decorated letters about boys, French and otherwise, and first kisses, French and otherwise. After reading and rereading each letter, and the postcards from Sonya's various holidays, I'd tack them on the bulletin boards I'd mounted next to my bed for that purpose. With Simon LeBon singing drowning out Mom and Dad's shouts, I'd lie on my bed and stare at the airmail stickers and postmarks, at the places I knew I'd go to as an adult, destinations already visited by a girl I knew I'd never really be.

The Pink and the Gray

Natalie, age 8

After the Barbies were abandoned and the playroom no longer had a purpose, it became my room. Shannon got our old room, which was quickly transformed to better meet her standards. New shelving was installed in her closet to accommodate her rapidly multiplying clothes and shoes. Caving into Shannon's repeated requests, Mom painted alternating walls pink and gray, with a special white bow border wrapping around them all, like a ribbon on a present. Shannon soon adorned the walls with carefully positioned posters from *Teen Beat* and *Bop*, of Duran Duran and Nick Rhodes, who she was convinced would someday marry her (or at least share her tube of pastel lipstick).

As I had outgrown the Vanity Smurf that Mom had painted on the playroom wall, my room was painted too—a solid light yellow, which I couldn't remember having picked. My living space was modest: a twin bed that once was Shannon's, a splintered vanity that had been my parents', and a few puppy posters stuck sloppily on the wall. The posters were birthday presents from classmates; I would have been too embarrassed to hang something of my own choosing, of which others might not approve. Though my room was quite unimpressive next to Shannon's, I would have been satisfied with my décor had I known about the addition that was to come.

When Shannon invited me into her room one day, I knew something was not right. She slammed her door after me, stormed to her bed, and plopped down. She didn't even say anything when I sat down too, careful not to let my bare feet touch her bed. She was silent for quite some time—longer, it seemed, than she had ever been. She just rocked back and forth, hugging her knees to her chin as she looked at her shoes, which she always wore in the house, for fear of soiling her socks. I didn't know what to do, so I stared at the hot pink flowers on her white jeans, then let my eyes skip around the rest of the room, once I'd realized my gaze had lingered too long. I looked up at her bulletin boards, cluttered with snapshots from sleepovers, postcards from Sonya, and letters penned by pals from around the globe. My few friends—who, like my shade of paint, I had not sought out, but simply found myself surrounded by—all lived within a fifteen-mile radius. I noticed the tapes stacked high on her dresser: Culture Club, Prince and The Revolution, and The Police, to name a few. I had only two tapes, which were blank because I lacked a tape recorder and the courage to tell Shannon what songs I liked.

"Mom's having another baby!" Shannon finally blurted, frantically running her fingers through her flopping spikes.

I didn't know what to say. "What?" I finally managed.

"Yep. Mom's pregnant. She's *been* pregnant for five months and didn't even bother to tell us. I can't believe it. I can't f-ing believe it!"

I just sat there, speechless.

I thought of our paper-thin walls, of a baby wailing over Shannon's music and Mom's clanking pans. I thought of Mom telling me, more and more nights, to call the bars and sweetly ask for Dad, to beg him to come home. (And I would have to do it, because even if Mom put on her most pleasant voice, "Toots" the bartender would lie and say he wasn't there.)

Even though Dad was gone most of the time now, our house seemed too small, our family too large. If there was not even room for me, how would there be room for a baby? The thought of Shannon being pushed into the background was unsettling, as well, simply because it would be different. Or would she stay at the forefront and would I completely disappear?

When I got back to my room, I cried. Mom did not accuse me having a "pity party," as she seemed to do every time I bawled about something Shannon got that I didn't, or something she was allowed to do that I was not. This time, I muffled my sobs in my slobber-stained pillow and even avoided my mirror. Usually, I would stare in awe at the sad-clown contortions of my face, my nose growing pink and puffy, and my lips morphing into a hideous frown. I did this even after the day Shannon walked in on me and ran, laughing uncontrollably, into the living room. "Oh, my God!" she choked, "Do you know what she's doing in there?" Now, I didn't need to see my sadness to believe it, and Shannon left me alone, though this time I didn't know if I wanted to be. I could even hear, on the other side of the wall, her own private "pity party."

The night my brother was born, it was storming. I don't know what woke me: the booming thunder, the lightning that lit up my naked window, or Mom thumping hurriedly down the hall. I sat up in my bed, which had been pushed to the corner of the room to make way for the crib that stood, waiting, where Vanity Smurf had been. Once my mind realized what my body already knew, I panicked, remembering that Shannon was at a sleepover and fearing that Dad wasn't home.

I was relieved when Dad pushed open my door. "C'mon, Nat," he said. "Mom's having the baby." Dad packed Mom and me into the car, and we rushed to pick up Shannon. Winding around wind-lashed trees and zapped power lines, we sped to Gabby's, where Shannon and I were dropped off. The next morning, Uncle Jerry came and took Shannon with him to the hospital. No one bothered to wake me.

I met my brother Neil later that day and got to hold him, though only while sitting down. I have two pictures of his first days at home, one of Shannon holding him (standing up), and me, reluctantly propped just inside the frame. It appears to have been taken post-pity party: I am slouching, my face is blotchy, and the corners of my mouth are anchored down. In the other, Shannon is again holding Neil, but this time her back is to the camera. I am standing next to her, almost shoulder to shoulder. My neck is stretched high, as if I am trying to reach her, and there is a forced grin on my face. In those days, such a smile was rare. I would glare at Mom every time she barged into my room to make sure Neil was still breathing. "Close the door!" I would yell after her, but she always kept it ajar. I pretended it was the lack of privacy that bothered me, but more than anything, it was the memory of when Mom used to check on *me*. When I was sick, she would make her bed on the floor next to mine, spooning medicine into my mouth at strict four-hour intervals, holding me up to cough, and slathering Vicks VapoRub on my chest through-out the night. She got up only to replenish my supply of toilet paper (facial tissue was a rare luxury for my family) or to refill the electric frying pan that served as my humidifier. Once she had even built me a tent of blankets.

Now, it seemed, the only reason Mom ever acknowledged my presence in my room was to give me instructions for watching Neil when she had to be away for a few minutes, and then to quiz me when she returned. I almost always complained, and sometimes threatened not to watch him, saying I didn't care what happened to him, that I wished he had never been born in the first place. (I had hoped this would make her reconsider having us share a room, but she never took the threat seriously.) Sometimes, however, after Mom was a safe distance down the hall, I would get up off my bed and stand over Neil, watching his breaths rise and fall. With him looking so innocent, it was hard to convince myself he had actually done anything wrong. After all, he hadn't chosen to be born. If I was sure no one was around, I would reach in the crib and touch his soft skin. Sometimes, I would even allow my lips to slip into a smile. Unlike the fake smile I had flashed for the camera, this one was me—sincere and erasable.

Ich...Is...Jeopardy!

Shannon, age 13

THE ONLY THING STANDING between the crown and
me was Dad.

"Dad, sit down!" Natalie and I screamed in unison. In our laps
lay college-ruled notebooks containing our final answers. It was a
close game, and Dad was blocking all twenty-five inches of our
Zenith television. For five consecutive evenings, he'd been coro-
neted with the *Jeopardy* crown. Made of the same paper on which
we tabulated our scores and committed our final answers, the
crown went to the reigning "*Jeopardy* Kring." If Mom won the
crown, she'd go and make dinner. If Natalie won the crown, I'd tear
it from her hands. If Dad won it, he'd perform what he called the
Jeopardy dance, which consisted of flailing his muscular, 5-foot-9
frame into jerky ballet poses. (This display resembled his Brian
Boitano impersonation, which he did around Olympic time to

divert Mom's attention from the television. When it failed, he'd tell her that Brian Boitano had pocks on his ass, a claim he made about Mel Gibson, Pierce Brosnan, and anyone else Mom fancied.)

On this evening, I prevailed, which meant that by the time Alex Trebek bid his viewers good night, I was waving at the losers as if I were riding on the back of a float. "Mirror, mirror, on the wall, who's the smartest Kring of all?" I taunted, smiling like a fill-in news anchor.

Although one might think that parents as intelligent as ours would go easy on Natalie and me during these games, they did not. We could hold our own in any battle of the brains: Trivial Pursuit, *Quiz Bowl,* the puzzles in the back of *Discovery* magazine. When we tired of these games, we invented our own. Our favorite centered around the local newspaper.

The Bee was twelve pages of weekly news so insignificant that it could wait until Tuesday. Sure, we got a kick out of the headlines: "25-MPH Low Speed Chase Ends in Field." "Breaking News: Heart Center Pulse Strong." "Vandals Strike Mailbox." But what really got us excited was the writing itself. Armed with red pens, Natalie and I would tear open the paper in a frenzied race to find the most grammatical errors and typos. Bonus points went to the sister who spotted the week's most glaring error.

"Look at this!" Natalie would say, holding up the classifieds. "'Spare parts for *truck's!*'"

"No, wait, look what I found!" I'd counter. 'Sheriff's Department warns seniors to stay in *there house* until temperatures drop.'"

Occasionally we'd have a draw, as was the case in a display ad reading, "Lose big $$$$ losing weight! Call to find out how!" and the one asking, "*Who'd* you know *want's* to buy a new car?" Finds such as these were added to a file of clippings we'd later use to make birthday cards for one another.

Natalie and I went about our childhoods confident in our mental capacities; that is, until our brother was born.

I was at Jenna Faufau's birthday party, mid-séance, when Neil's spirit, rather than Mary Worth's, materialized from beyond. Though I was, at age 13, revolted by the thought of how he came to be, I immediately loved him. Our first family photo, taken in Mom's hospital room, shows me in spiked hair and pink beads, Natalie with pity-party red eyes, Mom looking like she'd just been an unwilling participant in a sleep deprivation study, Dad wearing a grin the likes of which I'd never seen, and Neil looking like a breakfast sausage.

When he was a toddler, our brother's speech inexplicably sounded German. He even used the word "ich," though as Natalie pointed out, he used it in place of "this," rather than as a pronoun.

By age 2, Neil possessed a vocabulary roughly ten times that of the most literate *Bee* writer. By the time he was 3, his intelligence played itself out in his cataloging of birds he'd seen and fish he'd caught—complete with color diagrams, maps, and measurements. "Dad, I saw an Indigo Bunting yust yike ich vun," he'd say, pointing to a colorful bird in whatever gargantuan field guide he was lugging around at the time. Then he'd go off to draw his own version.

It was a bit unsettling to have a 6-year-old brother who could do math better than I, one who devoured my *The Ascent of Man* textbook during my college spring break and then briefed me on Pangaea, even drawing me before and after shots of the earth. This and every other bit of knowledge he amassed was cataloged, including his theories, which were followed by a neat question mark. Neil was a big fan of questions.

"Vhat's past the farthest galaxy?" he asked when riding in the car one night.

"I don't know," Mom answered. This was the safest answer, lest she wanted to risk being corrected by someone who couldn't take a bath without adult supervision.

"Maybe I'll find out one day," Neil said. At 4, he was already aspiring to be a meteorologist for NASA or the National Weather Service.

"Vhy are people afraid of skeletons?" he once asked me over dinner.

"I don't know," I answered.

"If zay knew zat skeletons gave us structure zay wouldn't be scared," he said, then took a memo pad from his pocket and scribbled numbers in it.

Even Neil's correspondence to me, which he dictated to Mom when I was at school, contained questions.

Dear Shannon,

Do you know what the biggest shark is? It's the Rhiniodon typus, commonly known as the whale shark. It can be up to 50 feet, which is 15 meters.

Do you know what the largest extinct shark is? The Megalodon.

Love,
Neil

Shopping for Neil's birthday and Christmas presents was easy. Anything a mad scientist would own appealed to him: microscopes, telescopes, test tubes and beakers, topographical maps, rocks. He, on the other hand, put a lot more thought into his gifts to us. One year for my birthday, he made me a forty-six-page book that illustrated the headdresses and clothing of each major North American Indian tribe's chief. It even contained a pullout map on which he'd drawn where the tribes had lived.

Mom assured us Neil wasn't "freaky" as Natalie and I pegged him.

"You girls were just as smart. When I volunteered at the school library that time, I thought the fourth graders were the special ed kids. Had I known better, I wouldn't have let them lick the chalkboard like that."

Neil eventually lost his accent but won the last *Jeopardy* crown. I'm pretty sure he still has it somewhere in his chest of drawers. If not the real thing, a diagram of it, filed under G for Game Show, right between Gagate and Gibson, Mel—Ass Pocks?

Raisin in the Sun

Natalie, age 9

It is said that you have to learn how to crawl before you can walk. Mom was afraid to let me do either, because as a baby, every time I tried to crawl, my arms would give out and I'd fall flat on my face. As a result of this infantile frailty, my mom carried me through the developmental stages during which most children are learning to stand on their own two feet.

Despite improvements in my body strength, Mom's concerns carried into my post-toddler years. Each time I attempted a new physical feat, if she allowed me try it at all, she would stand by nervously. After Dad had taught me how to ride a bike, Mom would station herself at the side door, its window pushed open in case she had to warn me of an obstacle, such as a dog on the loose or a rock she may have missed when she cleared my riding space. In reality, there was not much danger, since I was only allowed to ride on a small, flat patch of our yard, five feet from the window.

Some of Mom's other fears were more justified. Because I didn't know how to swim, she wouldn't let me in water any deeper than a bathtub. When we were at the park and I wandered toward the lake to watch the glimmer of the water, she would yell frantically, "Get away from there!" Since her fear seemed based on my inability to swim, I wondered why she didn't just have me take swimming lessons. I never asked her this because, as I soon figured out, I could use her restrictions to my advantage: they could assist me in getting out of social situations that my shyness prompted me to avoid. (Years later, Mom told me her reason for not sending me to swimming lessons: her cousin had drowned when Mom was a child, so Mom had developed an irrational fear of water.)

With Mom's history of discouraging extracurricular activities that required movement, I was shocked when she asked me if I wanted to take dance lessons.

Once I noticed Mom's hopeful smile, and the pamphlet she was holding, I realized this was not a hypothetical question.

"Where?" I said, confused.

"In Tomahawk. A lady just opened a dance studio, and she's looking for people to join."

Tomahawk, I knew, was the same town many of my classmates had gone for swimming lessons. I also knew that their classes had included kids from that town, as well as neighboring ones. I was certain dance lessons would be the same. I had my answer. "No."

"Why not, Nat? It would be fun."

"I don't know . . . I'd probably fall and get hurt or something."

Mom's smile dropped for a moment, then returned. "No, you wouldn't. How bad could you get hurt dancing?" It was a good question. I had danced at home many times and hadn't so much as pulled a muscle. Now I relied on Mom's other worry. Mom was not just afraid of my bones being shattered, but also my fragile feelings.

"What if I'm really bad at it? What if all the other kids make fun of me?"

Mom just chuckled. "Oh, Nat, you know that wouldn't happen. I've seen you and Lori dance before. You're as good as those dancers on *Solid Gold*." I knew she was exaggerating, but I also knew that what she was saying was partially true. If there was one thing I could be good at, besides drawing, it was dancing. Still, the idea of taking a class with a bunch of kids I didn't know terrified me.

"Okay, what if I told you Lori was going, too?" Mom must have been onto me.

As much as strangers intimidated me, the thought of Lori doing anything without me was even scarier. *What if she made all new friends and wasn't my best friend anymore?* I thought. Soon more unlikely scenarios crossed my mind, such as Lori rapidly surpassing me in her moves and, ultimately, trading my bedroom floor for a Madonna video.

Mom must have realized that I was seriously considering dance lessons. She immediately got on the phone with Lori's mom to confirm that Lori would, in fact, be attending. "Yep. She's going," Mom happily reported when she hung up.

"I guess I'm going, too," I said.

The dance studio was nothing like I had expected. It had no walls of mirrors, and instead of a barre, it had a bar, which gave tap-dancing a whole new meaning. The lessons were held at the VFW (*vee-ef-dubbya*, where I come from). The hall had been reserved, so at least its only patrons were moms in floral jumpers and the dozen or so little girls picking at the butts of their leotards. I walked in behind Mom and Lori, searching the floor for an inconspicuous place to put on my tap shoes, which I was horrified to discover the other girls were already wearing. Once the instructor greeted us, I felt much better. Terry had a big smile, bouncy hair, and a friendly, enthusiastic voice. Though her body was harder than any woman's I had seen, her instruction was the opposite. She seemed more like a mom to me than a teacher.

That day, I learned to shuffle, plié, and chassé. When Mom asked me which I liked best, tap, ballet, or jazz, I told her I didn't know. I liked them all.

For our first recital, I wore a shiny purple leotard with purple fringe, sparkly tights that looked like ladies' nylons, and a headband with a white feather whisping to one side. I had tried on the costume several times before the big day and practiced my tap dance in it, excited rather than scared by the thought of everyone watching me. My nerves kicked in, however, once I arrived at the school where the recital would be held. Not only was this a new place, but it was also full of girls I had never met. Mom walked me to the door leading backstage, and I reluctantly clicked down the hall, past moms kneeling before their daughters to cake makeup on their innocent faces. The finished product looked like pictures I had seen of Aunt Helen who, Gabby bragged, was a dancer in Vegas, and who Papa said was a stripper and a whore. I was glad no one had told me to bring makeup. But before I could find the rest of my classmates, one of the ladies grabbed my arm and began circling the apples of my cheeks with a tube of bright red lipstick. Afraid to protest, I let her paint my lips and poke a dark blue pencil around the rims of my eyes. When I looked in the mirror she thrust in my face, I felt more freakish than glamorous, but it was too late to wash my face. My group was being called to the stage.

As I waited behind the curtain, my knees began to tremble, and I wondered if I would be able to walk across the stage, much less dance. I looked over to Lori for comfort, but she seemed just as nervous as I.

After the announcer finished his long-winded introduction, silence fell over the crowd, and all I could hear were our unsynchronized taps like lazy horses trotting across the stage. All I could see was the black curtain in front of me, which I wished would never open, and then a bright light, like the ones area teenagers used to shine deer.

I could feel my legs shaking, my makeup melting down my face. I glanced at the large crowd and then did what Mom had told me to do. I stared at the blank wall in front of me, rather than at the faces in the crowd below. I listened to the music and tuned out everything but the sounds of my shoes. My limbs began to loosen, and my taps came as naturally as my heartbeats.

Afterward, Gabby bragged to her friends about how beautiful and graceful her granddaughter was. Mom called all of her friends to tell them I was the best one. Shannon was speechless.

Although I tossed the California Raisin suit I wore for the jazz dance and the Independence Day parade the following summer, I kept that purple leotard tucked in my memory box for years after I outgrew it. I would take it out from time to time, first to try it on, then as a fond reminder of when the bright lights skipped over Shannon and landed, directly, on me.

One Egg Short

Shannon, age 13

GABBY HAD, AT LAST, DISCOVERED THE SECRET of one-upping her sister Mary, and it would take just one egg.

"Oooh, Mary's coming, and I found a new recipe. One-egg cake, and oooh, is it good. Wait till she tries it! Just wait!"

It was a Saturday, and Natalie and I were spending the night at Gabby's, which Mom said we were now old enough to do unattended. The house reeked of bleach, as it did twenty-four hours before any of Mary's visits. The kitchen was completely free of clutter, with the exception of the Gerber jars of holy water on top of the microwave. Whenever Gabby dreamed of evil nuns, she stocked up.

"Does it have food coloring in it?" Natalie asked.

"No, no food coloring. You can eat it. Oooh, are you girls going to like it! Ta ta ta." Gabby wore a light pink shaker sweater, her latest find from a garage sale on Angler's Lane. Home to three of the town's four physicians, Angler's Lane was Gabby's shopping utopia.

As Gabby donned her apron to make a test cake, Natalie and I settled in for a night of television. As we were a good ten feet from the kitchen, we brought our provisions with us: hot chocolate, potato chips and dip, ginger snap cookies. By the time *227* hit the airwaves, we needed to restock. By the time *Hunter* ended, we could feel the food in our throats. I went to the kitchen to get water.

Gabby's back was to me, her hand shoved inside a jar of peanut butter. "I'm making peanut butter frosting, mmmm mmmm mmmm," she said, shimmying like she always did when she was happy.

Gabby took pride in her baking abilities, and I knew from Mom and Uncle Jerry's conversations that her baked goods—which she herself ate—were the only food she made that could be trusted when they were kids. When she used to prepare soup or a pot roast, she would lower her voice and say, "Oooh, I hope there's no glass or bleach in there," after they had taken a bite. She would then look through their food, and declare that she couldn't tell whether or not it was safe.

"Mary can't bake worth a damn! Hee hee hee," Gabby said, licking the peanut butter from her rubber spatula.

I chuckled, and the oven timer went off. As Gabby turned to open the door, she looked at me and gasped.

"Oooh, look at you! Look at you, big as a house!"

My smile left me. Natalie came into the room.

"Look at your sister!" she said to me, gesturing to Natalie. "She's Puny Harry. You're big like your mom. Just like your mom!"

Try as I might, I would never pass for Puny Harry, a glorious distinction shared by Natalie and a handful of cousins. Though I was not fat, I was not skinny and clearly did not take after my Dad's side of the family. I passed on the one-egg cake that night. I was already full of shame.

"Who threw up in my clean toilet?" Gabby demanded the next morning. "Mary's coming! I can't keep anything nice with you kids around. It's all mud. All mud!"

Gabby's foul mood passed as soon as she walked into the kitchen to make "Grandma's Perfect Pancakes" and caught sight of the last few pieces of her test cake. "Let's go to Hardee's for breakfast! Ta ta ta!" she said, doing a cha-cha in her new silver loafers, which no doubt had once belonged to Dr. Ferrar's wife.

The restaurant, one of only a few in town, was packed with seniors: seniors pumping ketchup into tiny paper cups, seniors tipping their heads to read the paper through their bifocals, seniors washing down dozens of pills with bitter coffee. They all knew Gabby.

We took the only open booth, at the back of the restaurant. Gabby asked if I wanted one or two sausage biscuits, and I said two. As she made her way up to the counter, she stopped to tell everyone that she was with her beautiful granddaughters. "Look how beautiful they are. Just look at them," she said in the same voice she used to boast her bingo wins. Natalie blushed, and I waved sweetly to her friends.

When Gabby returned, she handed Natalie a biscuit. As she went to hand me mine, she stopped. "You ordered two biscuits?"

"Yes," I said sheepishly.

Her face contorted into a sneer. "Look at this," she said to the family of four sitting next to us. "My granddaughter ordered two sausage biscuits. 'Get me two biscuits, Granny,' she begged. 'I want two biscuits!' Mark my words, she's gonna be big as her mom!" Ironically, it was not Mom's body I feared inheriting, it was Gabby's, which resembled a half-filled balloon.

The family smiled awkwardly and continued eating their pancakes. Gabby approached the next booth.

"Look at my granddaughters here. Natalie, the dark one. Oooh, isn't she beautiful. But look at my Shannon. She likes her food, yes she does!" She cackled, holding her hand over her mouth.

This time, I ate. I crammed both biscuits into my mouth, barely stopping to chew, and washed them down with my orange juice and Natalie's. As I did, Gabby bragged about her willpower, how she'd been eating nothing but cottage cheese and buttered noodles in anticipation of her sister's visit.

Mary arrived in the late afternoon. She had the same wiry hair as Gabby and a moustache.

As soon as Mary sat, Gabby began pointing out what was new in her living room since her sister's last visit. At best, Mary wrinkled her nose in response. At worse, she pointed out how her anniversary clock or doilies were better.

"Oooh, Mary," Gabby said, changing tactics. "I made a cake. One-egg cake with peanut butter frosting." She wore a sparkly tracksuit I'd never seen before and hurried into the kitchen to take out the second cake.

"Katie, you know I can't eat that. I'm on a diet. Look at how thin I'm getting." She smoothed her hands over her paunch.

Mary couldn't have eaten the cake even if she'd wanted to. When it emerged from the oven, it resembled a welcome mat. Mary snickered and went into the other room.

"I don't know what went wrong," Gabby said. Though she was looking at her cake as she said this, I knew she was talking about something more.

I didn't know what had gone wrong, either, but I knew it would take more than one egg to fix it.

Bingo Blood

Natalie, age 9

Gabby yanked my head back as she fastened an elastic tightly around my hair. "Oooh, wait'll those old biddies see my granddaughter. They'll just die!" she squealed. "You should see their granddaughters. Ugly as sin." After fumbling her fingers through the snarls in my ponytail, she danced around to face me, pressing my cheeks between her quivering palms. Just as the pressure became almost unbearable, she dropped her hands suddenly, her eyes widening. "Oooh, I know!" she gasped, tugging loose two tufts of hair just above my ears. "Oh, yes, that's it," she added, twirling the tendrils-to-be around her fingers.

Mom walked into the kitchen just as Gabby picked up the curling iron that had been heating on the counter beside me. "Oh, look!" Mom said in mock amazement, "You're making her look just like Scarlett O'Hara." Because I couldn't turn my head without the hot iron scorching my cheek, I squirmed slightly in my chair, hoping Mom would notice my plea for help. "Be careful with that thing, Ma," was all she said as she returned to her seat in the living room.

I was shocked that Mom had let Gabby put the iron to my head, and even more shocked that she was letting me go, without her supervision, to bingo. Although I was too young to participate in the highly acclaimed event Gabby called "The Big One," I enjoyed playing with the chips, wands, and daubers in her red vinyl "bingo bag." I also had played in two games at church festivals, which Gabby attended solely for gambling purposes. At one of these festivals, I'd won $9. Since that day, Gabby was convinced I had inherited her "bingo blood" and begged Mom to let me join the bingo circuit, wherever minors were allowed. Finally, after Gabby assured Mom that Betty—one of her few friends that Mom trusted—would be driving on this outing, Mom agreed.

Although Mom seemed okay with the excursion, I wasn't sure that I was, especially after Gabby pushed me in front of the mirror and I saw George Washington looking back at me. "Oooh, come on, let's show your ma," Gabby said, grabbing my arm and pulling me into the living room. When Gabby presented Mom with her new and improved daughter, Mom made no attempt to contain her laughter. Gabby must have mistaken Mom's reaction for uncontrollable joy. "Oooh, Sandy, doesn't she look beautiful?" she exclaimed, her eyes glistening with tears.

Before Betty pulled up in her Ford Tempo, Gabby propped me

among what she called her "Natalie dolls," which were lined on the floor beside her television. A Natalie doll was any doll with black or brown hair and brown eyes, regardless of her other features. Gabby purchased these dolls regularly, from her numerous doll magazine subscriptions or from the Home Shopping Network, which she called more frequently than any family member. Gabby also had "Shannon dolls," displayed on the opposite side of the room, on glass shelves scattered among haphazardly hung mirrors. I had noticed that, recently, my section had been growing rapidly while Shannon's remained stagnant. Now, with bright red cheeks and curls that bounced as I nodded, I agreed that I bore a striking resemblance to my porcelain and plastic counterparts.

Betty agreed, too, when Gabby asked her if I didn't look just like a doll. "Oh, yes," Betty replied, "that pretty little one in the blue dress." I was glad she didn't say I looked like Gabby's favorite, the life-sized one in the blood-red dress that frightened most visitors. Looking at that doll, I began to understand what Gabby meant by "ugly as sin." I figured Betty's granddaughters must not have fit into this category because, to my relief, she did not seem jealous at all. She even stood up for me when Gabby complained that I had refused to wear a dress. "Oh, Katie, she still looks pretty," she said.

Betty didn't seem like an old biddy at all. Her hair was brownish red, a more natural-looking version of Gabby's, and she drove remarkably well. Unlike Gabby, she stayed left of the shoulder and didn't jerk to a stop each time she had to switch gears. *Maybe this won't be so bad after all,* I thought as we pulled up to the bingo hall.

When we walked in, my eyes stung from the heavy cigarette smoke hovering in the air. I strained to see my competition, but to my surprise, there were no girls there my age. In fact, there didn't appear to be anyone even Gabby or Betty's age. The room was filled with white-haired senior citizens, many of them in wheel-chairs, parked along rows of metal tables. Each hunched over an expansive spread of bingo cards surrounded by neatly piled chips, accompanied by magnetic wands, or lines of assorted daubers. In addition to the bingo paraphernalia and numerous dirty ashtrays, the tables were decorated with what Gabby explained were good luck charms, troll dolls and rabbits' feet. "We don't need none of that," she giggled. "We got bingo blood."

As we made our way down the aisles, in search of vacant seats, Gabby tapped on the backs of those we passed. "This is my granddaughter. Look how beautiful she is." I kept my head down and hoped my hair had finally drooped. Most of those who were able to turn around simply nodded and smiled, except for a few men, who made earnest efforts to see me through their goggles. "Oh, yes, come here, you pretty little thing," one of them said as he reached out to touch me. I was relieved when the man sitting on the platform at the head of the hall announced through his megaphone that the games were about to begin. "Oooh! Hurry. Hurry," Gabby said, jerking me along by the arm of my jacket.

Once we were settled, and once I realized Gabby was the only one obsessed with my presence, I began to relax. After hours of games, my relaxation turned to boredom. Then suddenly it occurred to me that, if we continued to play game after game, there was a chance I would win one of them. Several meager monetary prizes had already been given, and no one at my table had yet won. Would I be the first? Though I liked the idea of having money to spend, I would give up any amount if it meant not having to yell "Bingo."

Whether it was bingo blood or increasing odds, my winning number was finally called. Everyone in the room, including even Gabby, was completely silent. Therefore, I thought, my declaration would not go unnoticed, even in this hard-of-hearing crowd. I decided pretending I hadn't heard the number would be ineffective, as Gabby scanned my cards after each number was called. I reached for a chip slowly, to buy myself time to think up a better plan, but it was no use. "You got it! You got it!" Gabby began convulsing. "Go on! Go on, say it!" she said, shaking my shoulders.

"Bingo," I muttered, so quietly I don't think Gabby even heard me.

"Bingo! Bingo! My granddaughter's got bingo!" Gabby stood up, flailing her arms.

I bowed my head, letting my tendrils work as blinders. I was relieved when the announcer said I could claim my prize after the next game, which would be the last.

"Oh, hurry up, ya old hags," Gabby whispered, spit flying from her mouth, as we shuffled toward the exit. "My granddaughter's gotta get her prize," she said, much louder, grinning down at me.

By now, I was smiling too, anticipating the envelope of money I was about to be handed. And the jealousy Shannon would undoubtedly feel.

When we finally made it up to the podium, I was glad that Gabby did all the talking for me. "Congratulations, little girl," the announcer said as he handed me a large box. Either this was a lot of money, I thought, or something even better.

I was terribly wrong. Inside the box was a deformed doll with a baby's face and a woman's body. "Well, look at this!" Gabby gasped. "Isn't she the prettiest thing you've ever seen? And look at that emerald dress. . . ."

I didn't have the heart to tell Gabby what I really thought, so I nodded in agreement.

When we got back to Gabby's house, Mom was still there, waiting to take me home. "Oooh, look what she won," Gabby proclaimed as soon as we walked through the door.

"Oh, yeah, that's nice," Mom said, flashing me a smile. Mom had seen enough of my Christmas and birthday wish lists to know I was opposed to any dolls that weren't Barbies. "Hey, Natalie, don't you think that would look nice *here,* next to the other—"

"Yes! Here," I said, handing the doll to Gabby.

After opening the box, adjusting the stand, and smoothing the skirt, Gabby placed the doll on top of the television. On her Zenith throne, the new Natalie doll stood above all of the others, even the life-sized one. She even towered over the Shannon dolls, standing on their shelves.

Gabby stood back, arms crossed over her chest, and nodded with approval. "Oooh, yes, I do think she's my favorite."

Wins and Losses

Shannon, age 13

YEARS BEFORE I'D STEP ONTO THE REAL THING, my stage was the fifty-yard stretch of asphalt just north of Tripoli Elementary's swing set and south of its parking lot. It was here that I discovered to the cheers and stunned expressions of everyone on the playground that I could not only run fast, but fastest.

The first time I was clocked, my phys. ed. teacher, Mr. Munson, scratched his red, glistening head as if there was actually hair there. "Kring," he said with a tone that could have been approval or disgust, "you take after your old man."

The only thing Munson was fast at was losing his temper. He took great pleasure in making girls in pink tennies cry, in throwing uncoordinated fourth-grade boys up against the wall or bleachers. When his watery eyes bulged like his beer belly, and his whistle began jumping up and down on his man-boobs, we knew to shut our mouths and quickly hurl whatever ball we were playing with—a dodge ball, a soccer ball, a softball—at the opposing team, and hard. The sight of kids doubling over in pain calmed him, to the point of laughter if there was blood involved. Munson had coached my dad and his two brothers, who were still revered for their athleticism. He agreed to let me run against the boys, all of whom I beat that day and every day after.

"Guess what, Dad?" I said, trying to play it cool when he got home from work that night. As usual when he got home, Dad limped slightly and was hunched over from having "beat himself into the ground" all day.

"What?" Dad asked, plunking his scratched lunchbox and Thermos on the snack bar. I wondered if he found it as awkward talking to me as I did him.

"I beat everyone in the fifty-yard-dash today at school. Even the boys."

"You're kidding," he said, his smile brilliant against his tanned face. He stood up straighter. "What was your time?"

"Five point six."

"Holy shit, that's good, Shan. Hey, let's go outside a minute," he said.

"Supper's almost done," Mom said, peeking into the oven.

"We won't be long," Dad said.

"Can I come?" Natalie asked, already scurrying toward her shoes.

"Sure, Nat," Dad said. "You got that Frisbee still?"

"Yep."

"Go get it! Let's play some Fris!"

We played Frisbee every night for a couple of weeks. Then one night, Dad brought home an aluminum bat. He always gave in when Natalie and I begged him to crack one across the road, past the neighbor's house, and out of sight, so he had to bring home new balls a few times a week. Dad and I stayed out until it was nearly dark and the mosquito bites made our legs resemble topographical maps.

My earliest memory of my father is not of his face, or of something he said, but the way he smelled in his polyester baseball uniform, salty and sunny, and the way his calves looked in his vibrant blue stirrups. I called them his jumping socks, believing that like Wonder Woman's cape, it was these socks that enabled him to jump so high. At the time, I was barely tall enough to reach up and knock on the snuff can in his back pocket before he flew out the door to play in another tournament in a town too far away for us to go. This, and the drinking Dad and his teammates did after each game, was the source of countless arguments between my parents, as when I was young, Mom would be left home alone to care for me. Miles away from the hospital or nearest grocery store, she did not have a car or license at the time, and lived in a perpetual state of fear while he was gone.

Dad played shortstop for a local team called the Jippos, but it could have been, should have been, the Yankees. Like many boys at the time, Dad had dreamed of being a professional baseball player, and in particular, a Yankee. Unlike most boys, he received an invitation from the Cincinnati Reds to attend their tryout camp when he was just 14 years old. (His parents said that it was too far to drive on such short notice—three weeks, plus he was just a kid—so he declined but kept the letter tucked away for years.) By the time he was a sophomore, scouts from the Chicago White Sox, Seattle Mariners, and Kansas City Royals had come to watch him play. When Dad was a senior, he attended a Pittsburgh Pirates try-out camp, after which the team expressed an interest in offering him a contract. Dad told them that he had plans to enroll in college, where he'd get much of the same experience as he would starting off in the minor leagues. A month after graduation, my parents were married. Dad started college in the fall, and in the winter, when he received his team tour schedule, it included three weeks of travel on the Gulf Coast. Deciding he couldn't leave my mother, who was struggling in her new surroundings, he quit the team (the same month I was conceived), and then quit school at the end of the semester. At 13, I did not understand why someone would pass up his dream, especially one that could have made him rich and famous.

"You could still play for the Yankees! Go do it!" I said once when Dad was grumbling over not having enough money to cover bills.

"I'm too old now," Dad said, staring at the game on TV.

But Dad, now 32, still looked like a kid when he'd dash out to his "beater" (Cug's dilapidated predecessor), turn the Yankees on the AM station, and lay across the front seat, his hands clasped behind his head, his ankles crossed. A sad kid, but a kid nonetheless.

In spring of 1986, Dad's and my common ground spread to basketball, specifically our love of the Boston Celtics and hate of the Los Angeles Lakers and Detroit Pistons. Cussing at Magic Johnson or Isaiah Thomas was a pastime that was ours alone, as Mom said the sound of sports on TV overloaded her circuits, and Natalie wouldn't dare call someone a "goddamn ball-hogging suckbag."

I didn't know if it was our hair color or something else, but our house had long felt divided between Mom and me, and Natalie and Dad. It's not that Mom and I shared interests that she and Natalie did not, it was that we could communicate without ever saying a word. Now that I was relating to my father for the first time, the house took on a different feel. Dad and I showed our solidarity by wearing Kelly green on each game day.

One afternoon during the playoffs, he suggested we go outside and race one another down the hill to the south of our house. It was my favorite hill to bike ride down, as it was steep and curved sharply to the right. "Sure," I said.

We walked past the foundation of what had been a general store when we first moved in. Tall grass grew up through the few floorboards that hadn't completely rotted away. The remains of several taverns that had mysteriously burnt down dotted our road, leaving no businesses on it. When we reached the top of the hill, Dad started stretching, so I did the same. We did this for a long time, and then Dad bent down, as if putting his feet into starting blocks. "Ready?" he asked.

"Yep."

"Go!" Dad yelled, hoarse from heckling the opposition.

Dad was fast! At first, I was able to keep up with him. When we reached the sharp turn sign near the bottom of the hill, however, he smiled at me and kicked it into high gear. I pumped my legs so quickly that it felt as if my knees would start dragging. Still I couldn't keep up. Natalie was already jumping up and down and clapping for Dad when I made it to the yard. Dad looked happier than I'd ever seen him. The next day, he was limping before he went to work, but he still challenged me to a rematch, saying, "That wasn't fair. I'll give you a head start next time."

He didn't. Though I made up some ground over the previous race, I was still the loser.

And then during the NBA conference finals, following Larry Bird's heart-stopping steal from Isaiah Thomas in the last five seconds of the game, and the subsequent victory dance that took place in our living room, he suggested we race again.

We ascended the hill in silence, and when we came to the top, Dad got straight into the starting position.

I don't know if Dad was slower that day, or if I was faster, but the first half of the race was a dead heat. As we rounded the corner, I imagined that I was back on the track at school, the kids clapping in time with my steps and chanting my name. I inched out in front of Dad, watching him out of the corner of my eye. I pushed harder and ended up a full two lengths ahead of him. And then I heard rocks scampering over asphalt, and a smack. I turned and saw Dad somersault on the road just as I made it into the yard. When I ran back to where he lay, I saw that his Celtics shorts were covered in blood. His right arm and leg were scraped and studded with pebbles, and his left shoe had come untied. When I tried to help him up, he winced and didn't look me in the eye. "I twisted my fucking ankle," he said, clutching his lower back.

Supporting his weight the best I could, we hobbled back to the house the same way we came, in silence. I hoped that Natalie hadn't seen the fall and that Mom wouldn't make a fuss over his injuries. I'd never felt embarrassment for my father before, and it paled only in comparison to the shame I felt for having beaten him. Somehow I knew it was more than a race, and that it was more than his daughter that had passed him by.

That summer, the Celtics lost to the Lakers in the finals. I went on to win the district track meet. When the NBA season started back up the following fall, I found myself caring less about Larry Bird's free-throw percentage and more about whether Kevin McHale or Danny Ainge was cuter. I set two eighth-grade track records, which I've heard still stand today.

My father and I never raced again, but if we had, would he have stretched first? Would he have tried harder? Would I have run behind him, or alongside him? Or might I have run at my own speed and risked surpassing him again?

That Game

Natalie, age 10

In addition to parachute pants and her period, Shannon got yet another thing I did not: a boyfriend. Lori and I were witness to this, as we hid, stifling our giggles, behind the strawberry bushes between our houses. Shannon and Mike were making out atop the bomb shelter, which Lori's grandfather had built, perhaps out of paranoia. Mom, definitely paranoid, warned us that it would cave in immediately if we stepped on or in it.

Not long after this, Lori and I got boyfriends, too. We began to play what we simply called "that game," which largely consisted of "making out" with Mike and Sean—that is, Mike Seaver from *Growing Pains* and Sean Astin, or "Mikey" from *The Goonies*, whose real name, I read in *YM*, was "Seen." We spent many summer nights with these invisible boyfriends, either at hotels (our houses) or in the camper that was parked outside of Lori's house in the summer. We preferred the privacy of the latter, where we could roll around undisturbed in our respective sleeping bags.

At least half of Sean's appeal was in his braces, which I imagined would taste something like a soda can, from which I would dreamily sip. I thought of asking Shannon what it was like, as her boyfriend had braces too, but we never spoke of such things (and, besides, it would give away my spying on her). I also liked Mikey for his asthma. I found something very appealing in the inability to breathe. I thought of it often, long after I stopped blowing into plastic Easter eggs and storing them in my closet, in case I should ever run out of air.

During my imaginary make-out sessions, I was not the shy and inhibited Natalie that I was in real life. I was Wendy Tellis, a rebellious, bubbly blonde. The story went like this: Wendy and her sister Heidi (Lori) had run away from home at 15 and 17, respectively, to live in the mansion of their rich Aunt Claire. This mansion, located in Sweet Valley, California—home of my favorite literary protagonists, the Sweet Valley Twins—was really the woods between our houses. We used tree stumps for chairs, swept leaves and pine needles to create "hallways," and laid sticks down—after breaking off the twigs for fake cigarettes—to outline "rooms." We sometimes pretended the trees were Mike and Sean, but they rarely visited us here, because the walls were invisible and if Shannon caught me, I would never hear the end of it. I would also run the risk of my dad seeing me hug a tree, which would have sent him into an outrage.

As much as I loved Sean, I loved Wendy even more. She was 5-foot-3, which I'd already surpassed, and a gymnast, which I was convinced I could never be, despite my success in the "tumbling" portion of dance class. As Shannon had once pointed out, I had neither the stature nor the guts to flip through the air. Lori's character was much taller, had long brown hair, and was very serious. This description could have matched me, whereas Wendy's could have matched Lori, who was giggly, yellow-haired, and a head shorter than I. I was considered pretty, Lori was considered cute, and we both wanted what the other had. Lori was tired of old ladies coming up to her in the supermarket and pinching her chubby, dimpled cheeks; I was tired of the same old ladies asking me what was wrong. I worked on expanding my cheeks at home in the mirror, transforming my usually sullen face into a toothy grin with, of course, braces, which I fashioned out of Juicy Fruit gum. When no one was around, I'd practice Wendy's voice, which was the squeaky, excited opposite of my low monotone.

Beyond giving me a boyfriend and an entirely new personality, "that game" offered something more: a sister who considered me not a nuisance, not merely an aide in her exploits, but a valued friend. Wendy and Heidi's relationship had all the qualities that Shannon's and mine lacked: They enjoyed being together, they shared their deepest darkest secrets, and they didn't envy each other in the least. Although I must have, on some level, wanted this kind of sisterhood, I never would have admitted it. In fact, Shannon and I often made an effort to show just how much we disliked each other, and it seemed that the only thing we agreed upon was that there was something wrong with sisters who got along. When we saw sisters hugging on TV, for instance, we would exclaim, "How cheesy!" or gag in unison.

In our house, this attitude was quite acceptable. At Gabby's house, it was a different story. Every time Shannon and I fought there, our tiffs caused the same reaction: Gabby's scarlet lips would begin to quiver as she stood rocking, her arms crossed tensely over her embroidered chest. "It hurts me when you girls fight," she would say. "It hurts me terrible." At this point she would begin shaking and shedding tears. "Oh, I regret the mean things I said to my sister. Oooh, I said hurtful things. Now Louise is gone and I miss her something fierce. One day, your parents will be gone, and all you'll have is your sister. Then your sister will be gone, and you'll have nothing."

After Gabby's speech, Shannon and I would immediately stop fighting—not because we saw any validity in her argument, but because previous incidents had revealed that if we didn't, we would next be urged to hug.

I understood something of what Gabby said once Heidi was gone. Wendy, of course, was gone, too, but that didn't make it hurt any less. Even long before Lori and I decided we were too old to play "that game," I had cried over its impending death. Just as Shannon's playing days were over, mine, too, would soon cease. I didn't *want* to stop playing, but I understood this was the natural progression of things, a loss beyond my control. I began to feel my imagination slipping away; I began to see Mikey as a cinematic character, my mansion as methodical trees. Even Wendy, whom I had worked so hard at being, was becoming someone far from myself. I was not happy with what and who was left; I wasn't even certain I knew what or who that was.

Once Lori and I finally quit—and we tried many times—it was even worse than I had imagined. What hurt the most, I realized, was not that I had lost my dream boyfriend, or even my ideal self. Most devastating was that I had lost the perfect sister. She had never really existed, but she was gone, and I missed her something fierce.

Secondhand Trident

SHANNON, AGE 14

MIKE DILLON was the kind of boy who made a girl forget all about germs.

A pubescent Robert Redford with braces and Bugle Boy jeans, he had the cocky swagger other eighth-grade boys would take years to master, though to be fair, his slightly bowed legs gave him two legs up on the competition. I first took notice of Mike while in the gymnasium, the middle-school version of the wine bar.

"Mmmm, look at Ben Peters," said Dawn. Ben tried unsuccessfully to dunk a basketball at the far end of the court. Seeing us eye him up, he flexed his biceps and winked in our direction. Loyal in her crushes, Dawn had for two years been pining after muscle-bound Ben, who wore tank tops even in winter. Not that I blamed her. Ben flunked second grade and was therefore more mature than the other boys. Plus, he was cute, if you looked past his chimp ears.

I didn't have the heart to tell her we talked on the phone for at least two hours every night and that he was, one year prior, the first boy to French kiss me. Dawn could have him, though. To me, boys were like fashion, and Ben was so last semester.

"Look at Jason," said Jenna. Jason and I had gone to grade school together and he was like a brother to me. Plus, he wore Wranglers.

"Look at David," cooed my best friend Becky. She liked bad boys, and David was no exception. He was a freshman with facial hair and a social worker. Before it was stylish, he wore head-to-toe black and referred to everyone, even teachers, as "dude." Though everyone knew he wouldn't amount to anything so grand, he aspired to become a tattoo artist and drew intricate dragons with ample-breasted women riding on them. Even his self-inflicted lighter burns were artistic.

"No, look at Mike Dillon," said Dawn.

Mike was jumping from the bleachers to hang by one hand on the rim. He was even svelte when his less agile friends tried to pelt him with their basketballs, dodging their attack and raking his fingers through his feathered hair at the same time. Another group of girls watched him from the other side of the gym, clapping like idiots when he stuck his landing.

"He has a butt like a sailor," declared Becky with an appreciative nod. I had no idea what a sailor's butt looked like, but if pokey-outey was the ass of a seafarer, then he had one, indeed.

"He's looking at Shannon!" Dawn squealed.

Nice eyes. Check. Arrogant grin. Check. New Nike Airs. Check. The ability to inspire insecurity and longing in other girls. Ding ding ding! We had a winner.

Mike cradled his basketball against his hip as he sauntered toward my bleacher, then smoothed his hair one last time before speaking. My friends scurried away.

"Hey, Shannon," he said.

"Hey." He smiled. I acted bored.

"Wanna go with me?" By going, he meant going no place in particular, but rather that he wanted me to be his girlfriend.

"Sure."

There was a school dance the next night, and when Mike kissed me during a Cyndi Lauper song, I was thinking about anything but the bacteria he might have had in his mouth.

For the next few weeks, I subsisted on a diet of tongue and secondhand spearmint gum. I began saving Mike's chewed Trident on my windowsill, and what started as a neat line of minty-smelling dots quickly grew into a fist-sized wad. By our two-month anniversary, it eclipsed most of the sunlight that once streamed in my window.

School began cutting into our valuable make-out time, so we were forced to ditch class to lock lips in the basement. I told the groundskeepers who played cards in the boiler room that we were brother and sister and wanted to be gardeners when we grew up, but that our parents insisted we become lawyers. In exchange for occasionally having to feign an interest in pruning and mulch, we had our freedom.

On weekends, Mike would spend the night at our mutual friend's house down the road, and we would meet at the graveyard. After making out on bags of topsoil, any location would do. When my lips could take no more of his braces, we'd walk hand-in-hand through the woods and carve "MAD + SRK = TLA" into trees with a jack knife Mike apparently carried for no other purpose.

Because we couldn't kiss over the phone, Mike and I discussed our future during hours-long conversations.

"How many cars should we have?" I asked.

"Seven."

"That's what I was thinking! Seven!" I pictured our seven shiny cars, each with a license plate reading *DILLON*. "How many houses will we have?"

"Two or three." I pictured our two or three houses, each with a mailbox reading *DILLON*.

"Say fish." I loved the way Mike said fish.

"Fish."

"Say dad." I loved the way Mike said dad.

"Dad."

Though being Mike's girlfriend boosted my popularity at school to an unprecedented high, my approval rating at home plummeted.

You have *got* to be kidding me," was Dad's reaction to my choice of first love. "Dinky Dillon's kid?"

My parents called Mike's dad Dinky, which was his nickname

when he was their high school teacher. It was hard to believe Mike's dad was old enough to have taught my parents, but proof was in the photo at the front of their senior yearbook. In it, Mike's father wore a V-necked sweater and neatly pressed dress slacks. His child-sized hands were clasped in front of his privates, and his hair was neatly parted and short. My dad, who wore Jesus-length hair and frayed bellbottoms, sat Indian-style on the floor, flashing his middle finger at the photographer. Dinky was now my eighth-grade civics teacher, and though my parents still snickered at his dwarf-like stature, I thought he was cute.

"But he's a *Republican,*" Dad said as if Dinky were a pedophile, or worse, a Jehovah's witness. (My father had no tolerance for conservatives or Christians, which explained his strained relationship with his mother.) Luckily, he took as much interest in my love life as he did in all other aspects of child rearing at the time and dropped the issue. I learned from Natalie's diary that she did approve of Mike and thought he was cute. She even covered for us one Saturday night.

"I'll be over in ten minutes," Mike had said on the telephone. It usually took him about an hour and a half to make it to my house on his BMX bicycle, but before I could ask if he was getting a ride, he said, "I'm driving myself."

I changed into a Guess T-shirt and applied bubble-gum-flavored lip gloss. Having been bribed with change I'd swiped from on top of the washing machine, Natalie distracted Mom with an impromptu tap-dancing routine, and I slipped out the side door.

Mike rolled into our unpaved driveway in his father's prized Volkswagen Jetta. Dinky spoke almost as highly of his car as he did of Reagan, saying in any lesson even remotely having to do with Germany, "The Germans built the Volkswagen to be every man's car. The name even translates to 'people's car.'"

What transpired that evening was legend by Monday morning. During homeroom, rumors of us playing chicken with a semi spread. Word of a high-speed police chase ripped through the halls by lunch, and by study hall, we were said to have totaled the car in an unfortunate incident involving a tanker truck. Reality, however, was more *Matlock than Dukes of Hazard.*

Because I lacked the foresight to have brought along a stack of phonebooks for him to sit on, Mike could barely see out the windshield; because of his heavy breathing and inability to work the defroster, I couldn't either. The good news was that at thirty miles per hour, there was a good chance Dinky would be drooling in a retirement home before we got caught.

We drove to Becky's house at a geriatric-like clip, Mike never once taking his hands from the steering wheel. When we arrived, it was not Becky who greeted us, but her father, The Shark. The Shark got his nickname not so much for his pro-wrestler frame as for his demeanor. He gave us a choice between calling our parents or "getting our asses kicked all the way home," so we took the former.

There would be other adventures—breaking into a cabin, lighting Mike's pants on fire while he was still wearing them, sneaking him into my room at night—but nothing matched the thrill of joyriding in Dinky's car. I foolishly believed the good times would last forever.

The demise of my planned eternal love arrived in the form of a sheet of college-ruled notebook paper folded into complicated origami. A mushroom? A hammer? A magnifying glass? One will never know. Unlike everything else to a status-conscious eighth grader, what mattered was what was on the inside:

Shannon,

The reason I'm breaking up with you is I feel trapped. I don't want to get caught up in a very serious relationship. To tell you the truth, I don't think I'm responsible enough to handle some-thing this serious. I think if we don't break up now I'll hurt you more later. It's not that I don't like you, I like you a lot. Don't think this is an easy decision for me. It's the hardest one I've ever made. I don't want you to hate me but you probably will. I hope we can be friends.

Love,
Mike

My chest felt as if it were being hollowed out with a rusty spoon, and I began what would become a nearly nonstop, four-week crying bender. I listened to Cheap Trick's "The Flame" over and over again and plotted to get him back. He did come back that summer, but in the role hideously, cruelly referred to as "friend." We tried walking in the woods, but without making out, there was really no point.

The following year, Mike began listening to The B-52s, music I would not have permitted in any of our seven cars or two to three houses. He began dressing in black and keeping the company of eleventh-grade girls with bad reputations. His grade point average dipped from a 4.0 to a 3.9, and it was rumored he smoked. He traded in his braces for a goatee, his tennies for steel-toed boots.

Still I watched him, and for years I compared every guy to him. To this day, the sight of origami makes me shudder, and the smell of minty-fresh breath makes me smile.

Dear Diary

Natalie, age 11

May 28, 1988

I was just thinking about Mike + me (as usual). This is different, now that the year has ended differently. In a new light, I figure, why be so sad and upset. Someday we'll be together, until then, we must say goodbye—not actually, those are the lines from our 7th grade graduation song. Anyway, why be sad. He brought something good into my life, and I miss my Mikie, but until (IF one day) we talk, I can't cry anymore. Just at night.

I read about Shannon's breakup with Mike more than a year after it happened. Huddled in my closet, I flipped through the gilt-edged pages, eating up all I could before Shannon returned from her friend's house. After gathering sufficient ammunition, I would stash it where I had found it, seven inches from the lower left corner of her bed, at an exact forty-five-degree angle. Shannon had changed her hiding place a week earlier, when she claimed the diary had been moved a centimeter from its place above our adjacent closets. I had discovered the "secret hiding place" when, writing *I [heart] Jeff* in chalk on a high, dark corner of my closet wall, I bumped my head on the ceiling, lifting the thin panel. I had spotted her diary then, but my fear and conscience would not allow me to read it. Plus, there was no key to accompany the gold lock.

Things were different now. Not only had I found the key, but I no longer had a moral obligation to respect Shannon's privacy. After Shannon had accused me of reading her diary, she found mine and did not hesitate to read it.

Unlike Shannon's diary, which was white leather with fancy gold lettering, mine was a stack of multicolored memo papers poked with a paperclip and tied together with string. On the cover, in black ink, was written "Diary," a detail I later regretted. It was hidden in a drawer of my vanity, under an assortment of mementos I had collected throughout the school year, including the plastic from a six-pack of Mountain Dew a boy had shared with me and a treasured "autograph book"—also a self-bound stack of papers—filled with *Stay Cool!* and *Have a Nice Summer!*, that I read over and over in search of hidden romantic meanings. In the diary itself, I documented the details of a life my family didn't know I had. As I became less popular at home—a trend I blamed on Neil and Shannon's continued existence, but that probably had more to do with my worsening attitude—my popularity at school reached an all-time high. I was not only liked by my teacher for my exemplary grades and good behavior, and by the girls for my tapered jeans and teased bangs (styles I had copied from Shannon), but it seemed the boys liked me, too.

I was in the fifth grade now and, because of the school's size, the fifth and sixth graders shared a classroom. To me, this meant one thing: more boys. Thanks to my sixth-grader cousin Sheilah—or perhaps because I was the only girl in the fifth grade known to wear a bra—the older boys began to notice me. Overwhelmed by my constantly changing crushes, I began to use my diary to explore my options: Jeff, the only fifth grader on my list, who smelled deliciously like pencils; Jerry, a rebel in camouflage pants and combat boots; and Billy, with an apple mouth of crisp white teeth and bold red lips that stretched all the way across his face. Although Jeff's position as the self-appointed president of the self-titled "Cool Fest" (a club of which I was proud to be a founding member) was certainly something to write about, another boy's crying in school or backing down to a bully could earn an entire page in my book. Even after I stopped stealing kisses from Andy Taylor in Shannon's Duran Duran poster, the least sought-after member of any group remained the primary object of my affection.

After Shannon had discovered all of my secrets, she delighted in sharing them with the rest of the household. She would strut through the house, taunting me with my own words: "Billy's lips were crusty today, but I still wanted to kiss him so bad!" "Jerry farted today. He is such a pig, but I think I'm falling in love with him." Mom would just chuckle and say, "Okay, Shannon, that's enough."

The first time Shannon had mocked me, I ran into my room crying, locked the door, and buried my face in my pillow. I was too embarrassed even to watch myself cry. I scribbled out all of my writing, then tore the pages into tiny bits and stuffed them deep into my wastebasket. I vowed never to leave evidence of my thoughts and feelings again. I also vowed to get even. I would read every incriminating detail of Shannon's life and tell not only my family, but everyone at school.

Now, as I flipped back and forth through the pages of bubbly letters in bright inks, bordered by hearts and Nike logos, I was determined to find the juiciest tidbits.

July 24, 1988: We unexpectedly had to go to town and I had to wear nerdy underwear.

September 3, 1988: Mike whipped a ball and pen at me. He had a snot hand today. Yuk.

I was obviously getting nowhere.

May 8, 1988 Mr. G caught Mike and me kissing. He is such a rude dude!

May 9, 1988: Mike and I kissed even before the bell. He Gandhied me in band . . .We probably kissed 24 times or so today.
Now I was getting somewhere. I didn't know what it meant to Gandhi someone, but it sounded pretty impressive.

Shannon would be home soon, but now I couldn't stop reading. One more page, I told myself, just one more page.

September 19, 1988: I am so upset because I lost the one thing in my life that was closest to my heart, that I loved, and if I wasn't such a pushy little bitch, he'd still love me.

I had never heard Shannon put herself down, and the only times I had seen her cry were when she was fighting with Mom—and then, I thought, only to get what she wanted. Maybe Shannon did have feelings, I began to consider. Maybe she didn't think she was as perfect as she pretended. Maybe, like our diaries, we were very different on the outside, but not all that different within.

I closed her diary and tucked it under her bed. I lingered there a while, imagining her lying there writing, and later, with the lights out, soaking her pillow with tears.

I never told Shannon I read her diary, nor did I tell anyone else. That night, when Shannon came home, she was wearing her usual structured blazer, Guess jeans, and loafers. She strutted past my room in the same cocky fashion, flashed me the same indifferent look. Nothing was out of the ordinary, but things were somehow different.

SEEING RED

TED STEVENSON lived in an immaculate ranch that stood in contrast to the other homes in our neighborhood, where double-mortgaged homeowners kept broken-down cars on their lawns for parts and rusted swing sets long after their children had moved away. The only thing that was ever on the Stevensons' lawn was their shiny riding mower, which was used nearly every day to keep their Kelly green grass crew-cut short.

Ted had been one of my closest friends since I painted a stripe down his tongue—which he stuck out at me in our third grade art class—in red tempera paint. We stood by one another through first dances, Flock of Seagulls haircuts, and even in our hours of greatest humiliation: when he threw up in front of the class and when I came in second at a track meet following my breakup with Mike.

I'd always regarded Ted as one of the girls, but the sophomore and junior girls obviously didn't. His ink-black hair made them swoon, and his dimples pushed them over the edge. I had my own gaggle of admirers, and Ted and I reveled in the attention of those sophisticated enough to smoke and listen to Metallica.

The afternoon before my fifteenth birthday, I'd been asked by my history teacher to write a speech to present at the Veterans Day program later that week. Ted had a set of encyclopedias, which his C+ average proved had gone unused, and that night my mom—who was once again, much to Natalie's and my horror, five-and-a-half months pregnant—drove me to his house to borrow the V volume.

Ted was on the phone with our friend Ben. They were discussing whether Stacy Hoffman's cup size was a C or D, and Ted handed me the phone and went to fetch the book.

"I told Ted there's no way they're a D," Ben said without saying hello. "Of course, I'd need to touch them to be sure."

"Like you guys have even seen a bra, Ben," I said with a laugh.

"Of course I've seen a bra."

"Your sister's and mother's don't count."

"Well, I've—"

"Nor do photos in magazines. Or in . . ." I trailed off when Ted entered the room and pulled down his Hawaiian shorts. He had nothing on underneath and, holding his erect penis in his hand, he lunged at me. I dropped the phone.

His eyes were glassy as he pushed me to the floor. He ripped at my jean jacket and dug his fingers into my breast with one hand, holding my mouth with his other when I began screaming.

"What are you doing? What are you doing?" I screamed, though the answer was obvious.

"I know you like it," he said in a voice lower than I'd ever heard from my friend. He laughed when I tried to free my arms.

What struck me about that moment were the scents around me: the sharpness of the carpet beneath me, the citrus-y soap on Ted's hands, and the brisk autumn air on my clothes. These were everyday scents, not the kind you'd expect at such a moment.

You're going to be raped, I thought. *Put your mind someplace else.* I stopped struggling and turned my face away from Ted, the carpet fibers rough on my cheek. Just as he succeeded in unbuttoning my jeans, heat began radiating in my stomach. My body felt like I was in the starting blocks at a race. I was a virgin and never imagined my first time like this. I was angry.

With strength I did not know I had, I struggled to free my legs from his and kicked him in the groin.

"Arrrr, you bitch. You're gonna pay!" he said after he caught his breath. As he poised himself above me, holding himself in his hands and sneering, I crawled crab-style on my back until I reached the hallway. I got to my feet and ran toward the screen door, through which I could see the headlights of our car. I heard him call after me but could not make out the words.

And then I was sitting next to Mom. The encyclopedia was in my lap, though I had no recollection of picking it up. My heart beat in my throat and I couldn't look Mom in the eye as the words and tears spilled out.

When we got home, close family friends awaited me with a birthday cake. As I sat on the toilet seat with the bathroom door locked, I heard Mom tell them what had happened. Tears made the room go wiggly, and when I closed my eyes, I saw the red flowers on Ted's Hawaiian shorts go spotty and turn the same shade as the sugary pink roses on my cake. I imagined the grainy pink frosting melting in my mouth and vomited.

There had been a note in the encyclopedia, we discovered later that night. "Here you go, babe," it read. "Thank you for tonight. I had a great time." Another note came the next morning, handed to me by Ted himself on the school bus as he passed my seat. His tight black words apologized for what had happened, saying that he was just so sick of everyone thinking he was a wimp.

When I got to school, I told my best friend what had happened and gave her the note. She gave it to the guidance counselor, with whom Mom had already spoken, and by second period, the sheriff had pulled Ted out of class. Mom picked me up from school, and that afternoon, the sheriff came to our house to question me. He brought Neil out to his squad car and turned on the lights and siren for him. Then he came inside and made me explain just how Ted had touched me, and I had to commit the horrible experience to paper while under his watchful eye. I told him I didn't wish to press charges, but I had no say. We were both minors, and this was now a state matter. I would be a witness in a case against Ted.

I went through with the Veterans Day speech, which I presented to the entire student body over a din of whispers and snickers. As I spoke, I was painfully aware of my too-curvy body, of the filth that couldn't be washed from it no matter how many times I bathed. For the first time in my life, I was envious of my sister's anonymity, of her ability to go through life unnoticed, never arousing the scrutiny that my every move seemed to bring.

In the days leading up to the trial, Ted's story was the one most of the student body accepted: He'd been about to get in the shower. The towel he wore slipped from his waist. I caught sight of him and forced myself on him. Ted took to wearing the look of a meek television character whose token line is, "Awww, shucks, ma'am." Girls took pity on him, and he started going out with a beautiful sophomore who ran cross-country. Those who believed me said I should have kept my mouth shut.

At the trial, I was asked if I had dressed provocatively on what the defense referred to as "the evening in question." I was asked if I had a crush on Ted, whether I had ever had sex, and to point to the area on my body where Ted had touched me.

"Please state for the record where you're touching," the prosecutor said.

"Between my legs."

"Where exactly between your legs?"

"My vagina," I had to say, with Ted and his parents looking at me from the front row.

Ted was found guilty and even caved and admitted what he'd

done, following Ben's testimony that he'd heard the struggle over the phone. But the records were sealed, and no one would have believed them anyway.

Ted's punishment was returning home immediately after basketball practice. My sentence, though self-inflicted, was harsher: starvation.

One month after the assault, Mom returned home shortly after Natalie and I got home from school. She handed Neil to Natalie and a box of Banquet chicken to me, telling me to make it. This was the first sign that something was wrong. We had never eaten dinner out of a box.

She went straight to the bathroom and ran herself a bath. I could hear muffled sobs from the other side of the door as I read the instructions for the chicken.

I wanted to ask her what was wrong, to comfort her, but all I could muster was, "I have to pee."

She did not respond, so I popped the lock.

The room was full of steam and she sat in the tub. She held her hands over the swell of her stomach and cried. *If we were a normal mother and daughter,* I thought, *I'd hug her now.* And then I noticed her pants, which were lying on the floor at my feet. They were bloody.

"I'm in labor," she said.

"I'll call Dad!" I said, turning around.

"Shannon, it's too soon. It's too soon," she wailed.

I could not reach Dad, and I felt helpless that I could not drive. My aunt rushed over to take her to the hospital, leaving me alone with Natalie and Neil. At ages 10 and 3, respectively, they were too young to understand what had happened, but old enough to know that something was wrong, and to cry.

I went to the bathroom and drained the tub, plunging my hand right into Mom's water. Then I picked up her clothing. I placed them in a paper bag and threw them in the trash, piling other trash over it so she'd never have to look at them again. Later, I dug the paper bag out and put it in the bathroom closet, way in the back, on the bottom shelf. *Would she want those clothes? Maybe she would want to throw them away herself?* I stood there a long time, debating whether to throw them back in the trash, when Neil came in.

"Shan-Shan, I'm hungwy," he said, putting his pudgy index finger to his mouth. He was still in his puffy blue snowsuit, his fine hair stuck to his head with sweat. I'd forgotten about the chicken, and when I opened the oven door, the heat made my mascara-coated lashes stick together.

Inside, the overcooked limbs screamed and writhed in their own grease. The smell filled me with a dizzying mixture of hunger and revulsion. For three weeks following the assault, I had had no appetite. Even when hunger had returned earlier that week, I'd refused to eat. *How can you even think of eating at a time like this?* I chided myself. *Mom won't eat tonight. Your unborn sibling may never taste food!*

"We aren't eating tonight," I said to Natalie and Neil, slamming the door shut. *And I'm never eating again,* I thought.

Two Hearts

Natalie, age 12

She was dead before I knew her, the baby Mom had carried inside her. After the baby was gone, Mom would spend hours sitting by the picture window, one foot tucked under her opposite thigh. She would absently pick her bottom lip as she stared out the window through the skinny trees across the street. I knew not to disturb her, because that would startle her, like when I woke her from one of her frequent naps and she jerked up and darted her eyes around, as though surrounded by a pack of hunters.

In the midst of one of Mom's moods, since I knew she wouldn't be getting up anytime soon, I searched the house for clues—to what, I wasn't sure, but I knew something was terribly wrong. Aside from Mom crying, which I had rarely witnessed before, other things had changed. Mom would go out at night and not tell us where she was going. When she was home and the phone rang, there was often a voice I did not recognize on the other end. I would pass her the handset, confused, and she'd offer no explanation or question who was calling. Greeting her caller with a whisper instead of her usually cheery "Hello," she'd shoo me away.

I began my search with the closets, which were consistently added to but never cleaned out. At first I found the usual: clothes that were never worn, Christmas presents Mom had forgotten about, books set aside for a rummage sale we never had. Finally I found something: a pamphlet that read "The Compassionate Friends." I opened it and saw little ink drawings of hearts and angels; poems with words like love, dove, and above; and pages of inspirational quotes on coping with the death of a child.

I showed Shannon what I had found, and she said, "Yeah, Mom's been going to meetings. It's a support group." She was in her room, sitting at her desk, hot-gluing some lace to the edge of a pink wooden heart. I was nervous watching her, as she had recently, by accident, glued her eyelashes together with the same gun. As I looked closer, I saw there were two hearts connected by twine. On the first, painted in silver, was "Kayla"; on the second heart, in identical writing, was "Lynn." I noticed that Shannon's calligraphy had greatly improved since she presented me with the "Worst Sister of 1988-89" award. Of course, I didn't share this with her. Once I registered that the names on the hearts were those Mom had chosen for her baby, I began to question why someone would make something—much less something so pretty—for someone who doesn't even exist.

"It's for Mom," Shannon said, noticing me gawking at the gift. "The Compassionate Friends say it's important to acknowledge the baby as a human being and the loss as a real one."

As much as I wanted to be compassionate, I could not understand how someone could grieve for someone they never knew, or why Mom would rather talk to strangers about "the loss" than to her own family. There were even simpler questions that had not been answered: Did the baby die inside Mom, or did it die after it was born? All Shannon had told me, after she'd answered the call from Dad, was that the baby hadn't made it. Did it resemble a real baby, or was it one of those shrimp-like creatures I'd seen in the video at school? I had only the guts to ask Shannon the latter question.

I was surprised by her answer: "She looked like a baby, just really small. She was premature."

"Like how small?"

"I don't know . . . Why don't you see for yourself?"

"Huh?" I was suddenly overcome with fear, as I imagined a mummified baby tumbling out of an opened closet.

"Mom has pictures. They're in her top drawer."

"Like from after she was dead?"

Shannon nodded.

"You saw them?"

"Yep."

"Were they gross?"

"Not really. She was kind of cute. But I don't think Mom wants you to see them."

"Why?"

"Because she's dead."

Weeks later, and several times after that, I sneaked into Mom's room. I would open the drawer, pull out the large manila envelope, and unwind the string. Then I would stop. I had never seen a dead person before, not even at a funeral. Mom and Dad didn't believe in open-casket funerals, because they said no one wants to remember someone, or be remembered, as they look when they are dead. Though I did not think of Kayla as my sister, I still didn't want to remember her, whoever she was, as a corpse—especially when I had no memories of her alive.

I never looked at those pictures, and of course, I hadn't seen Kayla at the funeral two weeks before. Sitting quietly in the small church, I had almost wished the casket was open, so maybe I could cry. I had thought about all of the sad things I could remember—all of my dogs that had died or run away—but no tears would come. That is, not until I saw my grandpa—who Mom once said had touched her only on one occasion, to rub her elbows raw with a vegetable scrubber—hug my mom after the service. Tears poured from my eyes, and I felt like I should hug her too. This, too, I couldn't bring myself to do.

The ground was frozen, so they couldn't bury Kayla that day. Months later, when spring arrived, Mom took us all to the cemetery to see the tombstone. I was surprised by the large plot of stones with my last name on them. I didn't know I had had so many relatives, and if I did, I wouldn't have guessed that they would all be buried in one place. When Mom spotted the stone that said Kayla, she pointed it out to us. It was much smaller and whiter than all the others and had a picture of a little angel on it. Shannon remarked how pretty it was, and how nice our uncles were to buy it. I didn't know what to say. I just stared at the small square of land, sprouting tiny sprigs of new grass, and tried to imagine this girl who never was. When nothing came, I thought about how I hated Shannon for her ability to think of Kayla as her sister. Not only that, but—judging from the crafts she had made each of us—she clearly perceived her as a better sister than me.

It would take a while, but I was eventually able to imagine pieces of who Kayla may have been. First, I thought about what she might have looked like. Would she have grown to have brown hair and brown eyes like me, or blond hair and blue eyes like Shannon? Would she have my long, skinny fingers and toes, or Shannon's short and stubby ones? Then I wondered who she could have been inside. Would she have been shy or outgoing? Submissive or assertive? Confident or awkward? Just as I was getting somewhere, I had this last thought, which slipped away as quickly as Kayla had slipped from this world—would she have been, could she have been, somewhere in between?

The Third Corey

Shannon, age 16

She would have been my second sister, Kayla, had she not been born too early. She lived only a couple of hours, and though Mom and Dad held her that night at the hospital, they'd made the decision to not let us see her, much less hold her. When he called from the hospital late that night, after she'd already gone, Dad said she looked like both Natalie and me—brown hair like Natalie's, blue eyes like mine.

The next few days were a blur, because I was too empty and too full, and because they passed in a seemingly endless procession of food. Uncle Jerry drove Kayla in her miniature white casket from the funeral home to the church. In the same car, he transported a platter of cold cuts and cheeses for the gathering at our house afterward. Someone would hug mom with one arm and hold a pale pistachio pudding-Cool Whip-cottage cheese concoction in the crook of their other. People cried, crunching potato chips through their tears, and I couldn't bear it any longer.

The only place people weren't was my parent's bedroom. I sat on the edge of their bed and saw the package the hospital had given them. Inside, Dad had told me, were a couple of photographs the nurses had taken of Kayla for them.

Kayla did look like Natalie and me, only skinnier. Far too skinny to be viable. What struck me even more than the similarity of her features to Natalie's and mine were her ribs and shoulder blades, the way they jutted out. *Her tiny arms,* I thought, looking at the shot of her lying on her side, *could have been no bigger than those Banquet chicken wings.*

Chicken was the first food I stopped eating. The very thought of it repulsed me, the way the veins snapped when the meat was pulled apart. Then I eliminated all meat. Next came oil, butter, and margarine. Then came pretty much everything else.

Classmates, even those who had very publicly supported Ted, began remarking how wonderful I looked. A teacher said that she was envious of my willpower. I became quite proud of this willpower, and secretly fearful that it wouldn't last. I began charting my achievements on a wall calendar of castles that someone had given me on my birthday. "GD," I'd write if it was a good day. This would be followed by a code that only I could read: number/number/number, which was my shorthand for number of calories, slash, fat grams, slash, and percentage of calories from fat on any given day. Over 900 calories or five grams of fat and I wouldn't use shorthand at all: "Bad day, PIG," I'd write in black Sharpie, and then spell out the words CALORIES, FAT, % FAT, a reminder of my failures.

Surprisingly, I looked forward to getting home and writing on my calendar. During the day, I'd keep track of my intake on tiny bits of scrap paper, and if that wasn't available wherever I was when I'd succumbed to the temptation of a single purple grape or sugarless stick of gum, I'd be forced to note my successes or failures on the inside soles of my shoes. Often, I did both, so as not to lose track of anything.

Scales, which I greeted with a mixture of repulsion and attraction, could prove only part of the story that my calendars could not. I developed other methods of charting my progress.

When Natalie was at dance class or in the living room eating—she was always eating!—I would sneak to her dresser and remove her clothes. She was 12 and skinny, and if only I could fit into her pants, I'd be a success!

At first, I could not pull them over my thighs. I'd jump and shimmy them, one leg then the other, over my calves, past my knees, and then to my lower thighs, where they would stop and remind me that I was a fat, disgusting failure. I cut my calories down to 500 per day, my fat grams to three, and eventually could get the pants past my thighs, then past my hips, and then finally to where I could button them.

Another way I charted my progress was to calculate how

much space was between my thighs while I stood with my knees together. One of Mom's empty diet soda cans was my instrument, until I realized that the can could dent and give me an unfair advantage. I moved to full soda cans, which I'd hold between my thighs, first vertically, and then, once I'd restricted my caloric intake even more, horizontally. This feat was achieved through my diet of five Saltines per day. I'd break them into pieces, chewing each bit fifty times while shaking my legs back and forth a hundred times to burn off the calories. By spring, I'd become so strong that one month, I'd only cheated once! I ate an orange Tic Tac at the end of the school day, for which I penalized myself two days' rations.

Although I reveled in my moral strength, I was getting weaker physically, unable to keep up with my late-night exercises, or to stay creative in hiding my starvation from others. Dad had begun calling me Bob, for Bag of Bones. He'd try to entice me with a bratwurst from time to time, or a burger off the grill. Even though he'd been softer lately, home much more often, he still kept his distance from me, something that at this point I was thankful for. Mom, still grief-stricken, would get out of bed only to see her therapist or to attend one of her Compassionate Friends meetings. Natalie was never home anymore, as she was always sleeping over at a friend's. My new boyfriend, Corey, however, was another story.

Corey was three years older than I and had moved in next door during my eighth-grade year. He was a senior and a headbanger, the leader of a somewhat feared group of older guys (mostly Corey's brothers and cousins) who hung out with their dirt bikes, ATVs, and Camaros at the gravel pit, thrashing their mulleted heads to the screams of Metallica, Anthrax, Slayer, and a host of other non-British bands who therefore didn't find their way onto my stereo. These guys drank, smoked, and cussed their way into bad reputations and the dirty fantasies of my squeaky-clean girlfriends.

As if we hadn't gotten a good enough look at Corey's Greek god-in-tight-Levis physique when he strutted through our wing of the school, my friends and I would spy on him after school with Neil's high-powered bird watching binoculars: Corey in a muscle shirt splitting wood in the yard. Corey in a muscle shirt lifting weights in the garage. Corey in a muscle shirt working on his car. Pretty much the only time Corey wasn't wearing a muscle shirt was . . . never. And pretty much the only time I wasn't observing his biceps in said muscle shirt was when I was with Mike. Even though we'd broken up, he'd still come over occasionally, and wherever Mike was—if it was near me—Corey was not far behind. If Mike pedaled up on a bicycle, Corey roared in on a motorcycle. If Mike was hanging from the large oak on the edge of the woods, Corey would back flip into the yard. If Mike got within twelve inches of me, there'd be Corey, suddenly flexing in a muscle shirt between us. Not coincidentally, the last time Mike came over, just before we began high school, there was an incident involving whatever sports car Corey was rebuilding at the time. I was in the house and missed the majority of the scene, but it ended with squealing tires and Corey's shouting, "That's right, little boy," out the window to Mike, who scampered from my stoop like a squirrel being chased from a birdfeeder by a menacing pit bull. As my first love pedaled into the sunset, never to be seen within twelve inches of my house or me again, I was enraged. I hated Corey! Hated his horrible music! Hated his bullying! Hated his headbanger vernacular, especially the incessant use of *them* in place of *those,* of *poser* in reference to anyone who wore shirts with sleeves!

But soon, the very muscle flexing I loathed began to take hold of me, first figuratively as Corey moved his pec-pumping operation out of the garage and into plain sight, and then literally as he began stopping in when I had a girlfriend over and doling out tight goodbye hugs. Serenaded at my bedroom window by lyrics such as *On your back look on to me/You'll see genocide/ Face from death more than insane/profane pleading cries/Watch you die inside watch you die* that blared from his new Pioneer stereo and equalizer, no doubt an entire month's wages from his work as a carpenter, I got to thinking: Maybe big boy headbangers weren't *so* bad. They were just . . . different. Dating one would be like having a boyfriend and bodyguard in one. I'd get to ride on the back of a motorcycle. All of the adrenaline and testosterone would probably be thrilling. Maybe it would even be effective in making a certain "little boy" jealous. Plus I wouldn't have to borrow Neil's binoculars anymore. Brilliant, or so I thought.

Corey and I officially became an item just after Kayla's death.

Jessica and Sara were the first I told.

"What? You and *Corey* kissed? Hot Corey?" Jessica squealed.

"He's like 19, isn't he?" Sara asked, darting her big eyes around the hallway as if it were Cold War Russia and the poster-clad lockers were spies.

"Eighteen, I think, but so what?" Jessica said, slapping Sara's shoulder. "Give it up, girl," she said, eagerly awaiting the juiciest of details. Jessica had just arrived from Chicago and had shamelessly indulged in the fruits of the headbanger tree on more than one occasion.

I told her how Corey had kissed me on my front steps. Yes, French. Yes, he was wearing the really, really ripped jeans. Yes, the ripped jean jacket too. Of course a muscle shirt under it. No, he didn't feel me up. Yes, I was pretty sure he would soon.

This, the feeling up part, was something that made me nervous. Not because he'd be the first to do so, but because since the assault, I didn't want anyone feeling me up, down, or any other direction, especially since I'd started my starvation regimen. Would Corey notice that I'd been starving myself? Worse, would he not?

At the gravel pit, where the guys went *mudbogging*—driving their vehicles of choice at full speed up and down the snow-, sleet-, or rain-soaked embankments—most of Corey's sentences started with *fuck* and ended with *you*. But at his house—where we hung out most and he lived with his parents, younger brother, adult brother and sister, and her daughter—they often began with *please* and ended with *ma'am*. Corey's mother ruled their roost with a pudgy fist, and in stark contrast to our house, filled with self-help books and silence as of late, her home was filled with pastries and commotion. If she and Corey's sister weren't baking and laughing, they were baking and bickering. Cake-from-scratch afternoons punctuated by scratching-your-eyes-out catfights were commonplace, and I loved every second of it.

Up in Corey's room after school, we'd explore one another under the covers with our clothes and Guns 'n' Roses on. Eventually, he did feel me up, and it was clear that whatever it was he thought of my body, it was good. Below us was the familiar clank of pots and pans, and just over his shoulder, out the steamed-up window, was my family's house, barely visible in the fading daylight.

Several months into our relationship, Corey traded in his current rebuilt car for a shiny, new pickup. As Northern Wisconsin social mores at the time dictated that the size of a man's penis was directly proportionate to the size of his tires, I found myself in auto supply stores, from which he purchased a lift kit that suspended the truck off of the ground in monster truck fashion, tires half my height, flaming-red shocks, roll bars (black metal bars that were mounted behind the truck cab to protect one in the event of a mudbogging snafu and, more importantly, looked "tits," the headbangers' highest accolade), and a muffler that purposely made his truck sound like Cug.

One afternoon, I agreed to climb up in the truck to ride to the nearest city, an hour away, so that Corey could purchase a special hammer for use at his carpenter job. He neglected to tell me this excursion would take me to Fleet Farm, a gigantic brown-and-orange metal building that smelled of rubber and housed everything from farm-animal feed to bras to canned cashews. When we emerged an hour and a half later with a hammer and a few more embellishments for his truck, I asked Corey if he would venture into my world: the mall. Here, surrounded by pop Muzak and racks upon racks of un-ripped jeans, Corey appeared as uncomfortable as I was around farm implements. But we went back the next weekend, and the one after that, which proved his love for me more than *any* muscle could. Slowly, trips to the gravel pit were completely replaced with ones to The Limited, and as I grew my own wardrobe through his generosity, I talked Corey into considering attire that would cover his appendages. Eventually, he was looking more like one of the "original" Coreys—Haim or Feldman—than he did himself.

My parents liked Corey, and he liked them. So much that he once invited Mom outside to put her Kenny G on his truck's new tape deck. The three of us sat in his truck under the stars—with the windows tightly closed, of course, lest someone hear anything but heavy metal coming from the cab—and it was the first time in months that I'd seen Mom smile. Shortly thereafter, when Corey and his family had a falling out, my parents invited him to stay with us. He packed a few belongings and soon began building a bedroom in our basement. No one noticed that this did not make me smile.

Cover Up

Natalie, age 12

Spike was long gone. Before I knew what had happened, she had been replaced by a girl in low-cut V-neck sweaters, Spandex tank tops, and skintight leggings. Whereas Spike had freckles and transparent-lashed pig eyes, the new girl's complexion was even-toned porcelain, her light blue irises glistening inside dark fringes. Her short, boyish spikes had flopped and lengthened into fluffy tresses, and her taut, mean grin had transformed into a pretty pastel pout. Instead of beating up boys, she was batting her newly curled eyelashes at them.

Mom liked this Shannon. I measured her affection by the hours they spent together in the bathroom, painting their pallid faces and curling their limp blonde hair. "Hurry up!" I would yell from the living room, ready in my rumpled Hanes T-shirt, baggy ripped jeans, and wet tangled hair (if I was lucky enough to get into the shower before their ritual began). After school had let out for summer, I saw no reason to look pretty. Even when I had cared what I looked like, my beauty regimen—1. Drench bangs in Aussie Scrunch Spray. 2. Sizzle under curling iron clamp. 3. Rat and repeat.—had taken place in my room, behind a closed door. Besides, I knew my disheveled appearance bothered Mom and Shannon, inspiring me even more.

When Mom and Shannon finally emerged from a cloud of hairspray, we would ride thirty miles into "town," Shannon in the front seat with Mom, and me, of course, in the back. The whole way, they would share beauty tips or talk about their problems, such as the devastation of humidity to their makeup and hair, or how opening the window of our air-conditionless car could cause the deconstruction of their 'dos. Although they glanced often into their mirrors, to make sure nothing had fallen or smeared, they failed to see me rolling my eyes in the background.

After getting past my initial annoyance, I was usually able to stare out my window and daydream. Soon I was no longer in the car with two strangers, but on the school bus with Jerry, reliving my first kiss. I could still taste his saliva, tinged with Mountain Dew and sour cream and onion potato chips. I had felt a special sense of intimacy when a piece of chip dislodged from his tooth and found a bed in one of my many cavities. After he changed buses, I was delighted to carry a piece of him with me, and now I had a good reason not to brush or floss, something Mom and Shannon did until their gums bled.

I told neither Mom nor Shannon about my new boyfriend. Mom would have told me I was too young, and Shannon would have ridiculed me in front of her friends. Besides, Shannon had recently befriended Jerry's cousin Corey, who surely would have told both his family and mine. Shannon and Corey had been spending more and more time together. Driving by on one of his 2-, 3-, or 4-wheel vehicles, he would swerve into our yard immediately upon seeing Shannon. For hours they would stand in the grass, now as ripped as Corey's abs, which I could see through the giant cutout beneath his armpit. I knew something was going on when I went outside one night to catch fireflies and saw them sitting atop our hill, Shannon wearing his slashed denim jacket patched with Anthrax and Slayer logos. His arm was around her, partially covering the "Metallica" written across the back in black Sharpie.

Soon, Shannon began wearing her jean jacket more often, and holes and large splotches of bleach began mysteriously appearing on her jeans. She would play "Sweet Child of Mine," over and over, and songs that screamed lyrics I was embarrassed to hear in her presence. At first, I was happy. I liked Corey, and I thought Shannon's change of appearance meant she would lighten up a bit on mine. Contrary to my belief, her criticisms only intensified. Now, when I wore the slashed jeans I had even before Corey came along, Shannon accused me of wearing them to copy her or to impress Corey. As if that wasn't bad enough, she would add—in front of Corey—that I had better start shaving my legs, because hair was beginning to poke through the strings that stretched across my knee. Soon, I began to wish Corey and Shannon would break up, and I was certain that Mom would be the one to make that happen. I knew Mom hated heavy metal, and I strongly suspected she would think Corey was a bad influence, too old, or a combination of both.

I was wrong. Mom loved Corey, and she loved the fact that Shannon had a serious boyfriend. Now, on our trips to town, makeup tips—which were still prevalent—led to relationship advice. Their talk did not subside once we arrived at the mall: "Mom, do you think Corey would like this?"

"Yeah, but I was thinking this one."

"Well, you could just buy both . . ."

Although Mom didn't mind that Shannon was in an adult relationship with an adult, I thought that based on Cliff Huxtable's interrogations of his daughters' boyfriends on *The Cosby Show,* surely my dad would. Again, I was wrong. Not only did Dad think Corey would make a suitable mate for his daughter, but he also foresaw that Corey would make the perfect fishing mate for himself. Now Dad had someone to talk to about things like motors, as well as someone to do all of the home improvements he had neglected. With Corey moving in, we didn't just get a new family member; we got new siding over our house's chipped blue exterior, homey bricks over the grease-splattered space above the stove, and tiles to cover the steam-soaked holes in the bathroom floor. Neil got the quintessential playmate. After Corey moved in, our living room became a Nerf basketball court, filled with balls of all sizes (that I frequently had to dodge) and Neil's squeals of glee. Neil adored Corey so much that he even asked to get his hair cut just like him. Mom was more than willing to pick up her shears and master the mini mullet.

With the new addition to our household, the house seemed more crowded than ever. Now, I didn't have to fight Mom and Shannon for the bathroom; I had to fight MomandShannonandCorey for the bathroom. I didn't just have to drown out Mom and Shannon's giggles penetrating my bedroom wall; I had drown out those of MomandShannonandCorey. Our outings were no better: Despite there being only two seats in the front of our car, MomandShannonandCorey always managed to squeeze into them. Shannon and Corey couldn't use the backseat to kiss, because Shannon claimed to get carsick. The lovebirds' smooching was enough to make *me* sick.

Like Shannon's headbanger phase, the honeymoon didn't last long. Shannon and Corey still got along okay, as far as I could see, and although my parents began viewing Corey more as a family member than a celebrity guest, they continued to love him. Still, something was wrong. I just couldn't say what.

Shannon started dressing more like Shannon again, as did Corey. Shannon had picked out a sweater for him at a men's clothing store that sold suits, and he now wore it often. Shannon wore a lot of sweaters, too. But these days, instead of being hugged by cashmere, her torso was wound in a giant ball of yarn. Her sweaters, or sometimes blazers with heavily padded shoulders, always reached just above her knees. If her sweater rode up when she sat, she would quickly tug it down over her legs, which now resembled knitting needles. She continued to wear a lot of makeup, but instead of pinkish blush, she brushed on bronzer, which seemed to deepen the valleys forming under her cheeks. On her lips she wore an opaque, dark brown, which she reapplied often, though she rarely ate or drank.

With her appearance, Shannon's relationship with Mom also changed. Although their moods always seemed to coincide, they were not the team they had been before. Instead of seeking relationship advice, Shannon would frequently slam her door in Mom's face when Mom attempted to mediate an argument between Shannon and Corey. This was quite a change from months before, when, after a blowout, MomandShannonandCorey all smiled and cried to "This Heart Needs a Second Chance" in the front seat of the car.

Mom and Shannon also fought frequently about food. Although Mom had accepted Shannon's vegetarianism in the beginning, it now seemed to anger her. Once, when Shannon refused to eat the meatless meal Mom had prepared just for her, Mom flung the wooden spoon across the room, screaming, "For Chrissakes, Shannon, just eat some goddamn spaghetti!" Another time, Shannon threw a slice of pizza onto the ceiling rather than putting it in her mouth. "I'm not hungry!" she exclaimed, her voice shaking.

I was confused as to why Mom was so mad. I had noticed only a slight change in Shannon's weight, and I thought it made her look better rather than worse. But then I remembered all the times Mom had gotten ready or peed in the bathroom when Shannon was in the shower. Maybe Mom had seen something that I had not. More likely, I told myself, she was just being paranoid again.

Our car rides, too, began to change. Corey usually opted to stay home or go fishing with Dad and Neil. Now, instead of just going shopping, we would also go to the Lutheran church, where Mom and Shannon had their "Shirley appointments." They never told me exactly what went on while I sat in the waiting room, paging through badly illustrated books with stories about forbidden apples and boats as crowded as my house. But I could tell from their red eyes when they came out of Shirley's office that the meetings were not pleasant. On rides home, Shannon and Mom still talked about their looks, but only until they thought I had fallen asleep. As soon as I closed my eyes, their conversation would turn to other topics, like what they called "The Ted Thing." They never said what "The Ted Thing" was, but rather spoke around it, using phrases like "since The Ted Thing." They would go on to discuss equally vague topics like "control issues" or whatever concept Shirley was teaching them about at the time. Whatever The Ted Thing was, I knew it was sad, because every time they talked about it, their words were punctuated with sniffles. As soon as I stirred in my seat, they would comment on how their allergies were acting up, and their conversation would return to makeup. As curious as I was, a part of me felt relieved when this happened. I even began "awakening" on purpose. I knew that makeup covered more than just their faces, but I wasn't ready to find out what.

Detached

WHEN NATALIE CALLED ME A DRAMA QUEEN, it was an insult. But when Mr. Abney, my forensics and drama coach, called me one, it was on par with being called "Dame" by the Queen of England.

Abney was pipe-cleaner thin and dressed like a TV professor, complete with corduroy blazers with suede patches on the elbows, and thin, V-neck sweaters in drab colors. A native Virginian, he was considered somewhat exotic in our neck of the woods, what with his pronunciation of the word *wash* ("worsh") and his having read Shakespeare.

Abney had been my Advanced Placement history teacher in eighth and ninth grades; in the latter year, he gave me the lead in the spring play, *The Night of January 16th*. In it, I played a smartly dressed woman who was standing trial for the murder of her boss and lover, Bjorn Faulkner. When I asked him if he believed that I'd offed Bjorn, Abney replied, "What you are or aren't, only you know. What you make the audience believe may be something altogether different from the truth." We understood one another, and Abney pushed me as hard on the stage as he did in the classroom.

The following year, Abney cast me as the ditzy sister in *Cheaper by the Dozen,* and I got the laughs. The year after that, when he announced *Charlotte's Web* as the spring production, I knew that lanky, 6-foot-tall-senior Pam would snatch the role of Charlotte. Even with my warped body image, I could see that there was a host of girls who'd better qualify to play Wilbur the pig. When I approached him about the play not being one in which I could showcase my talents, Abney clutched his clipboard to his concave chest and nodded.

"Perhaps you should take it easy this year, Kinky." He had called me this since eighth grade because of my hairdo, which took an hour to create with a sizzling crimping iron and several layers of Vavoom! hairspray.

"Take it easy?" This was the man who praised me for getting up at 3 a.m. to study on test mornings, and who told me I was getting sloppy when I had scored "just" a 96 percent on an exam. "What do you mean?"

"Do you know what a tachometer is?" he asked.

"No."

"It's an instrument that gauges the rotations of the shaft. Most old cars used to have them, and when you pushed a car too much, the pin redlined. That's what you're in danger of doing right now. You're pushing it too hard. You're redlining."

The next thing I knew, I was cast as Goose—not Greta the Goose, nor Gary the Goose—but as a barnyard animal so unimportant, it didn't even warrant a name.

But I had other problems. Now down to three Saltines per day, I found it impossible to stay awake during the first few nights of practice. I had two recurring dreams: being force-fed Bac-Os, and being trapped in the backseat of a moving car with no driver. *Hadn't Mom just been driving? Where did she go?* Both dreams caused me to awaken terrified, and with a headache larger than the one I had when I'd fallen asleep. No matter how long I'd slept, I was depleted.

My only energy came from the brief rush I'd get after passing one of the many "tests" I'd give myself throughout the day—joining my friends in the cafeteria as they ate lunch, selling candy as a fundraiser, keeping a sandwich in my locker. (Never once did I cave!) I even took home ec, where I spent my afternoons baking pies and pastries, and microwaving cheesy cauliflower and gooey caramel corn. This late-afternoon class afforded me the greatest test of all: would I fail and lick a batter-covered spatula, or would I have the determination to tough it out? On my weaker days, when I'd catch myself eating vicariously through my classmates, I'd run my creations down to my geometry teacher—burning even more calories!—as a bribe for overlooking my slacking in class, and as a way to get temptation off my hands.

And then one day, the dizziness and headaches took their leave. With hunger now past me, I lacked any sensation. I cradled the hollowness I felt in my core as if it were my child, a precious gift that filled me more than any amount of food ever could. So when I told Abney I quit, and he seemed disappointed—even though it was he who encouraged me to cut back on my activities—I didn't care.

My friends, apparently clueless about how many calories were in beer, had long given up on my accepting their invites to their many parties. Only a handful of girls spoke to me anymore, mainly those who were onto my "dieting" and thus wanted to know the secrets of my success (It's simple! Just don't eat!). Apparently, others were catching on, too. Once, when entering the locker room after phys. ed., I overheard a small group whispering about me: "Little Miss Perfect thinks she's so great because she doesn't eat a carrot." "No kidding. I think she's doing it for the attention!" Sara, one of my closest friends, sat with them. She didn't laugh like the others, but she didn't defend me, either. At last, I was the topic of every conversation, and this was the sentiment? Fuck them all.

Corey tried to brighten my spirits with gifts and sweet kisses. Though I did not have the heart to tell him, the last thing I was interested in or capable of was physical contact, and especially with him. Though I at first enjoyed having him stay with us, this too became a source of shame for me. The fact that I was living with my boyfriend was the other dirty little secret that pulled me further and further away from the seemingly carefree lives of my peers. Plus, he was nice to me.

One night, I agreed to go to a movie with him and eat some licorice. The licorice part was a promise I had no intention of keeping, and thanks to the enemy—my body—I had the perfect excuse.

I stood in front of my mirror, examining my legs in the olive green and black paisley leggings. Something had changed. *Did the gap between my thighs become bigger, or am I getting fatter? God, probably fatter! Where did that soda can go? It was just here!*

Teary because the walk down to the kitchen trashcan—where Corey had no doubt chucked my secret thigh-measuring tool—was too far a trip, I grabbed the silk shirt from my bed and lifted my arms over my head to put it on. When the pain came, all air left my lungs. *Did I get stabbed?* I wondered, gripping my chest as I fell to the floor. No sound came from my mouth as I tried to cry out. Or maybe it did, because Corey and Mom were pounding on my door. It was locked, as it always was during my body critiques.

Corey must have broken the door open, because then I was at the hospital where I'd been born. The doctors and nurses seemed frantic, as they moved about me, attaching various pads and tubes.

"Has she recently been seriously ill?" a nurse asked Mom. "Her skin is pasty, and she's very thin." *Cool, I must be losing weight*, I thought.

"Well, she's not been eating. She has anorexia, but no one will listen to me." A few weeks earlier, Mom had taken me to see our new family doctor. After running tests, he assured Mom that most of my numbers had fallen in the low-normal range, and that there was nothing to worry about. Feeling like a failure, I nearly stopped eating altogether. Now, at long last, my hard work had finally been recognized!

I woke up at home the next morning. Natalie was sitting in front of the TV, nervously picking her bottom lip. I was lying on the couch. My first thought was, *Why would they put a metal rod under the cushion?*

It was not a heart attack, nor was it a metal rod. It was my rib cage, which had, because of a loss of muscle tone, become detached from its normal position, after we had done archery in phys. ed. earlier that day. There was a long name for it, and my doctor said he had read that Michael Jackson had the condition. Despite strong anti-inflammatory medication, I looked like I was wearing a life vest. I could not lift more than a glass of water, and it was possible I'd never be able to participate in normal physical activities. I'd been lucky, they said, but I didn't feel lucky at all.

"You're going to see Shirley, starting this week, Shannon," Mom said, looking every bit as frightened as she did when I was a child and sick. Part of me wished I were still a little girl so she could make me all better. "And you're going to start eating!" she said, gripping my forearm. So much for that.

It had been years since I'd been in a therapist's office, and this time, I had a hard time slapping on a smile. Mom and I had fought the entire way to town, while Natalie sat in the backseat with her eyes closed.

"I just need to lose five pounds! Five more pounds and then I'll be happy! Please, just five pounds and everything will be okay!" I screamed. Every time I had this thought—that I could stop after five more pounds—I believed it. The problem was, there was always another five pounds after it.

For a moment, she was quiet and I thought she'd give in. But then she said, "No, Shannon, you're getting some help."

Some help? Try a lot of help, Mom, I thought when I entered the office. Shirley was a large woman, one I believed could stand to skip a meal or two herself. Her arms clasped around her pillowy waist, she had a legal pad resting on her thigh and began our session not with the lecture I had anticipated, but with a smile and a "So." She told me she was glad I had come, that she'd heard a lot about me. She told me she'd been a ballerina, that she'd struggled with eating problems much of her life. Then she started asking me questions, the kinds that as a kid I'd envisioned Barbara Walters asking me. I was on a heavily padded couch, flowers and Kleenex beside me, and allowed myself to settle in for the fans watching at home. Then she asked something that made me snap out of fantasyland.

"Your mom was abused as a child, Shannon."

"I know. I feel bad about that, but it's not like I had an easy childhood." My words were tough, but I felt anything but. About a month earlier, Mom had told me the truth about her past—a truth so horrible that it took Kayla's death to shake loose the most horrific memories—I could think of little else. Gabby had been the woman I'd read about in Mom's letters years earlier. It was she who had chased my mother with knives and who had done so much worse. I tried to envision the woman Mom had described, and the image was so far removed from the ditzy grandmother of today that it baffled me.

Shirley poised her pen to her temple. "Do you think you were abused as a child too?"

I thought back to Mom's hyper-vigilence about leaving me alone with any adult but Dad or Jerry. To never being able to attend sleepovers at homes Mom deemed unsafe. To her declaration that food left out for more than twenty minutes was "bad." Now I understood. "No," I answered. "I was the opposite of abused, but the effects are the same."

"And what are those effects?" I could not answer, because I suddenly felt like crying. "Let the tears come," she said.

The effects would take several more sessions to explain, but the tears did come that day. When I left the office, Mom didn't look at me with expectancy, and I didn't try to hide my tears. She patted my arm and looked like she was going to cry, too.

We stopped at Kentucky Fried Chicken on the way home.

"Did you eat today?" Mom asked as we stood in line. She already knew the answer.

"No," I said, too drained to lie.

She ordered an individual mashed potatoes and coleslaw for

me, a three-piece chicken dinner for Natalie, and a diet Pepsi for herself. Mom never ate in public, and at home, I rarely saw her eat anything that didn't come out of a bag. Now this, too, made sense. "Let's sit so you can get some calories in you before we head home," she said.

When she took the lid from the potatoes, the smell made my stomach churn. I initially thought it was because of the smell—which was like an outhouse—but maybe it was something else? Could hunger have returned? And even if it had, could I allow myself to give in to it?

No.

"Jesus Christ, Shannon, just take one bite!" Mom pleaded after sniffing the potatoes and announcing them fine. "How hard is that?"

"I can't. My stomach is sick."

"It's because you're hungry! Just take a bite! One bite! I guarantee you'll feel better!"

I remembered going to Kentucky Fried Chicken as a kid, before Natalie and Neil were born. It was always on the way to or from something special, like fireworks on the Fourth of July. I'd sit in the back seat, the air from Dad's open window making my hair fly like sugar in a cotton candy machine. Mom would sing to the radio, and Dad would try harmony.

"I can't. I just can't," I said. Mom grabbed the spoon, and I swatted it out of her hands in a panic. "No, you can't make me!" I said, shrieking as if she were trying to feed me a squirming rat. The cashiers looked to our booth, and I saw us through their eyes, a young woman throwing a temper tantrum, an older woman sobbing as she tries, and fails, to spoon-feed her. A pre-teen staring down at her plate as she practically inhales a chicken thigh. We drove back home in silence, Mom and I detached from one another in every way but our tears.

Physical therapy and dietician appointments were added to my weekly psychotherapy appointments, which meant I was all but pulled out of school. Physical therapy was painful, as was everything from low temperatures to coughing, as both and nearly everything in between caused a tear in my chest, prompting another trip to the emergency room. I hated the dietician because she spoke only of eating, and because she did so as if I were slow: "This. Is. The. Food. Pyramid. See? Do. You. Think. *You.* Could. Eat. Two. Pieces. Of. String. Cheese. This. Week? Hmm? Do. You?"

I couldn't eat the two pieces of string cheese, nor the yogurt she suggested. Sure, I went to the silly appointments to get everyone off my back, but I was not about to give up starvation. It was the one thing I had to cling to.

Still, Mom would buy the string cheese, yogurt, and other items the dietician had outlined in my weekly meal plans.

"Did you eat that yogurt today?" she asked me one night, as I walked past the kitchen to go out with Corey. I did not answer her. "Did you hear me? Did you eat that yogurt I gave you this morning?"

"I forgot."

"You forgot? You forgot. Well, you can forget going out tonight."

"Whatever," I said, walking toward the front door.

"You're not leaving without eating! I got those granola bars, and some—"

"I'm not hungry!"

Mom blocked the front door. "Kerry, please help me!" she said to Dad, who was watching the news. "Kerry, do you hear me? She didn't eat anything again today, and she's not going out!" Dad didn't respond, and unable to move Mom from the doorway, I walked to my room as fast as my weakened legs would carry me.

"Kerry, would it be too much to ask for you to give me some help with your daughter? She's not listening! Kerry! You hear me? Help me here, will you?" I could hear Mom yell from the living room.

Planning to jump out my south-facing window as I had done to meet Mike what felt like a lifetime ago, I popped out the screen just as Mom barged through the door.

"What do you think you're doing? Shannon, you're going to eat something!"

"I am not!" I screamed, stretching my leg up toward the windowsill. I felt a sharp pain in the middle of my back. *How would I lift myself up?*

Mom grabbed me around the waist and pulled me away from the window. I hit her fingers and kicked her shins. She cried out as her glasses fell to the floor, and then tightened her grip. "Shannon, get away from the window! You've got to eat! Please!"

She grabbed my wrists, and I twisted under her arm as if dancing. "Just let me go!"

"I can't do that," she said, her voice shaky.

"Why don't you just leave me alone? Just leave me alone! Why are you so hard on me?"

"Shirley says pity kills the anorexic, Shannon."

We were both sobbing now, and my curtain and rod came crashing down on us. Mom sighed and let her arms fall to her sides.

"All right, Shannon, go if that's what you want. I'm done arguing with you." She left the room and returned to the kitchen. I just stood there. Torn between thinking people were making a big deal out of nothing and wishing they'd save me, I didn't know whether to stay or go. I went, and I spent the night in a haze.

And then one night, coming back from a movie, I caught my reflection in the side mirror of Corey's truck. I was yawning. *That's me?* My hair was dull, brittle, and thin. My face was . . . skinny. No, not just skinny. Skinny like a skeleton, my cheekbones jutting out, and cords of skin holding my open mouth in place.

Until that moment, I had never seen myself as others did: as dying. The girls who used to be my friends weren't staring at me out of jealousy, they were gawking out of fright. When Gabby told me I was getting too thin (though never Puny Harry), she meant it. When Mom told me I'd kill myself if I didn't start taking my therapy seriously, she was right. As denial took its leave, fear stepped in to fill the emptiness. *What if it was too late?*

My recovery was a slow process that truly began when Mom

and I had a joint therapy session, during which Shirley explained that we were unhealthily "enmeshed." This meant that Mom saw me as an extension of herself and that because she so identified with me, she believed I needed extra attention so as not to suffer like she had as a child. She explained to Mom that in her quest to make my life better than her own—and to give me the self-esteem she lacked—she tried to make my life perfect. Because I viewed Mom as an extension of myself, I didn't want her to see any behavior or emotion that she may perceive as failure on her part. Shirley said that this caused me to hide my sadness, and, because I also felt guilty for experiencing joy when Mom was in the midst of depression, to also hide my happiness. To me, it seemed wrong to feel bad when Mom tried so hard, or to feel good when she felt so bad.

Mom explained how hard she'd tried to prevent me from having the sadness and fear she'd experienced as a child.

"You had everything! You got everything you wanted, clothes we couldn't afford, everything!" she cried to me.

"And do you know how guilty that made me feel? Me having all these clothes, and you dressing in rags?" Mom, who owned one pair of tattered jeans, two T-shirts, one bra, and a couple of ratty pairs of underwear, started crying. But I continued. "If I don't come home happy every day, you get all shook up! And then you get depressed, like you failed! So I keep it all hidden!"

Mom sobbed, and Shirley pointed out how she hadn't failed at all, that she was a much better mother than her own mother was.

"And now you can let me take over," Shirley said, putting her arm around Mom and leading her to the door.

Not long after our session, Mom confronted Gabby about having abused her as a child. That isn't what she set out to do, that evening in October, but that's what happened.

We were on our way to town to grocery shop, where Mom would zip down each aisle, nervously adding prices in her head as she filled the cart with anything she thought I'd eat, and, at least for now, anything that wouldn't require refrigeration. Our refrigerator had died, right along with the balance in Mom and Dad's checkbook, so for the past six days, Mom had compulsively checked the Styrofoam cooler sitting on the back steps to make certain the ice hadn't melted, turning our mayonnaise into Salmonella spread that would kill her babies by nightfall.

The day the refrigerator conked out, we'd stopped at Gabby's so Mom could ask her if she knew of anyone who had a refrigerator for sale. Gabby and her friends were constantly selling their wares when they won big at the casino, or to make some quick loot so they could go back when they weren't as lucky.

"Oh, damn it," Gabby had said. "Who was just saying they had a fridge to get rid of?" And then she remembered, "Imogene. I'll call her today. She won't ask much, either. Fifty dollars, I'll bet you could get it for. She'll sell it to me cheap if I say it's for my daughter. She likes me."

Eager to see Uncle Jerry, whose car was parked out front,

Natalie and I piled out of the car and raced around Mom to get into the house. Papa was in the backyard, scaling fish in the fading sunlight. We didn't wave, and neither did he.

When Mom got inside, she stopped, staring in disbelief at the clean, white refrigerator that sat where Gabby's harvest gold fridge—the one she had just five days ago bragged about still working like new—used to be.

Gabby giggled. "Oooh, I like this fridge better. It matches my stove, not like that old yellow thing I had."

"What did you do with yours?" Mom asked, her voice steamy.

"I gave that old thing away. You wouldn't have wanted it. It was harvest gold."

Mom and Uncle Jerry exchanged glances, and I knew they were thinking the same thing I was. It was always like this when Mom was in need of anything. The month before, when Mom's purse strap broke, and Gabby noticed the leather knotted around the metal ring to keep it on Mom's shoulder, she said, "Oooh, look at you, you need a new purse!" Two days later, Gabby appeared with a new one—chocolate leather with butterscotch-colored piping, just the style Mom would have bought, if she'd had the money. Gabby kept the purse for just one week, saying she didn't care for it, and then sold it to a friend, buying a beige, straw style with flower appliqués running up its sides to replace it. When the zipper had broken on Mom's jacket, or when the heels of her shoes started looking like cakes baked in an unleveled oven, Gabby would run out to buy herself a jacket or two, with matching shoes. She'd not wear them, but would simply cram them into one of her already brimming closets after modeling them for Mom. Mom should have expected the same thing to happen with the refrigerator, but just like every other time, she seemed shocked all over again.

I expected Mom to pack us in the car without a word to Gabby, and maybe stand next to the car with Jerry for a while, spouting off about Gabby's gall, before driving home in silence. But she didn't budge. Apparently, it was one thing for Gabby to acquire the "luxury item" Mom needed for herself, but a whole new ballgame when what she needed was a necessity to keep her children healthy and well fed.

"You kept the fridge Imogene was selling to me, for yourself? When you know I've been without one for nearly a week?" Mom asked. Uncle Jerry grumbled under his breath.

For once, Gabby was speechless, and stood fidgeting next to her new TV. Everyone was silent. Mom looked over at Natalie, who sat scowling on the orange couch that made the room look like Halloween. "Go wait in the car, girls." Her voice told us not to buck her on this one. Natalie sighed and headed out the door first, which was good, because I was able to inconspicuously leave the entry door open, after letting the screen door slap shut, so that Mom would think we were gone.

I tugged Natalie toward the tree where Papa's bird feeder hung. Through the screen, we had the perfect view. Gabby, in her pink sweatshirt with Holly Hobby on the front, picked at her chin with nervous fingers, her eyes as wide behind her glasses as the actresses' in the slasher movies she loved. Mom stood with her back to us, her fists balled.

"You did this on purpose!" she screamed in Gabby's face. "You know how badly I need a fridge, and you did this just to show me that I don't deserve a damn thing! You've always done this!"

"What are you talking about?" Gabby replied. "I've always been good to you. I've always been good to you kids."

There was nothing funny in Mom's laugh. "Good to me? Are you kidding me? You beat the shit out of me when I was a kid! You chased us with knives and threatened to cut out our hearts! You let me know every day of my stinking childhood that I didn't deserve a damn thing but what you dished out to me!"

Gabby shuffled like she was doing the jitterbug. "I, I couldn't help it. I was sick back then. I didn't know what I was doing."

I leaned over to see where Uncle Jerry was and was glad to see him standing near Mom.

Gabby's lips started quivering then. Mom moved closer to Gabby, leaning over her. I remembered that when I was little, Gabby was almost as tall as Mom. Now Mom towered over her. "Save your crocodile tears," she spat. "There's no one here to see them, and they don't work on me anymore!"

Mom glanced over at the heart-shaped wreath of black silk flowers that Gabby had recently hung over her couch. It matched her new black drapes and black wallpaper border. "Is it any wonder," Mom continued, "that you have the dreams you have?" I knew what dreams Mom was referring to. I'd seen Gabby wake from a nap after having one of them: her recurring nightmare in which the Virgin Mary loomed over her on the horizon, pointing an accusatory finger in her face. Two weeks ago, Gabby had claimed that it was the Virgin Mary herself who told her to start going to church, and when I asked her why, she said, "I don't know. To repent, I guess." That's when Mom told her that she'd better hurry, because at her age, there weren't all that many Sundays left. Mom had then said that Gabby had a black soul, and that if she were her, she'd head to church and wait on the steps until the door opened. Gabby only laughed then, but afterward, she started decorating her house in black.

Mom lifted her arm and pointed at the wreath. "God, how sick is that?"

Gabby's face contorted into an expression I'd never seen before. It was as dark as her decorations, only uglier. Her stature changed, and her hands stopped shaking. Natalie took a step forward. I grabbed her arm and whispered, "Hey, don't let Mom see you," even though I suspected at this point that Mom had forgotten that we were even there. Natalie shrugged herself free and shushed me.

When it came, Gabby's voice was an eerie rumble. "So what if I have a black heart. Maybe I like having a black heart!" Her words may have scared Natalie and me, but they didn't scare Mom. Mom only dipped her head until it hovered just inches from Gabby's upturned face. "Now get out of my house, you bitch," Gabby said.

Mom didn't budge. "No. Not until I've said what I should have said a long time ago!"

"Get out!" Gabby hissed, her eyes, dry now, rolling back into her head.

"What are you going to do? Beat me? Run for a knife? I'm not a little kid anymore, in case you didn't notice, and you can't hurt me now. I'm not afraid of you anymore, Ma. You got that? I'm not afraid of you anymore!"

Gabby looked afraid, now. Her face sagged, and she turned and half-ran, half hopped, out of the room like a toddler, her voice little-girlish as she shouted, "Daddy! Daddy!" to Papa like the house was on fire.

Mom moved from one leg to the other. Even though we were several feet away, with the screen between us, I could hear her breaths.

Papa came through the back door and entered the living room, his metal fish scaler still in his hand. "What's going on here?" he demanded, his face etched with trouble.

"Oh, Daddy, you should hear the things she's saying to me," Gabby cried. "How I was mean, and—"

"*I* never laid a hand on you kids!" Papa shouted, as though he'd been accused. His hands shook, snowing shiny scales onto the carpet.

"No, you never laid a hand on me! Wait, I take that back. Once, when I was little and Ma had left you again, you noticed that my elbows were dirty. You brought me to the sink and scrubbed them with a vegetable brush. You touched me that one time in my life, to scrub my elbows till they were raw, so I wouldn't shame you by being dirty. Other than that, you just walked away, and let her beat the shit out of us, and scare us half to death!"

By this time, Gabby was wailing, swabbing at her crinkled, rouge-colored cheeks. "Make her leave, Daddy," she begged Papa.

"Get out! Right now!" Papa boomed, and then backed Mom toward the door. Natalie and I hurried to the driveway and hid behind the car. Natalie looked stunned, and I realized that the truth about Mom's past must have come as a shock to her.

Mom paced in tight circles on the gravel driveway. Uncle Jerry stood next to her as she cried. She turned toward the car, and then paused, heading back to the house, where she pounded on the door with her fist. "I'm not finished!" she bellowed. "Goddamn it, open this door!" The door must have opened a crack, Gabby or Papa saying something that only infuriated her more. "No! I'm not leaving until I've said what I have to say! You can open the door and let me back in, or let me stand out here and scream it for the neighbors to hear. Take your pick!" There was a pause, and then Mom shouted, "Go ahead, call the cops! Maybe they'd like to hear what I have to say, too!" The door opened, then, and Mom and Uncle Jerry went inside, slamming both doors behind them.

I didn't hear the rest of the conversation, and I didn't need to. As the sun dipped beneath the garage and Natalie and I braced ourselves against the autumn breeze, Mom didn't once peek her head out to see whether or not we had zipped our coats, or even if we were still in the yard.

Something shifted in our mother after that day. She stopped being so afraid, even of me dying. Shirley was right. Mom had been a far better mother to Natalie and me than Gabby had been to her, and it was ultimately her tough love that led to my recovery. From that day on, she did her best not to comment on what I was or wasn't eating. I did my best to feel, and to let those emotions show. Together, we struggled to bridge the gap between what we showed the audience and what was real.

Other Peoples' Messes

Natalie, age 12

I didn't know the exact cause of Shannon's injury, nor its severity; but I was sure it would turn my life upside down. I convinced myself of this as soon as Mom told me I would have to carry Shannon's book bag for her until she got better. While I considered the extra weight enough of a burden, I began to panic as I imagined how ridiculous I'd look, carrying two humongous duffel bags onto the bus. And what would I say when the kids asked why? Not even I knew the answer to the imagined question.

"But what will I tell people?" I asked Mom.

"Just tell them the truth—that your sister hurt herself in gym, and she can't lift her bag."

Without having been told, I knew this wasn't the whole truth and, for some reason, the thought of saying it made me uneasy. I was afraid to ask what the whole truth was.

"Are you sure she can't lift it?"

"Yes."

"Can't someone else do it?"

"No, you're the only one who can carry it onto the bus."

"But what if—"

"Natalie, you can do this for your sister."

I gave up, somehow knowing that, unlike a lengthy grounding sentence, there was no way of getting out of this.

The first day wasn't as bad as I'd anticipated. Mel—our jolly bus driver—greeted us with his usual smile and "H-hi, Shannon. H-hi, Natalie."

When he saw that I was carrying Shannon's bag, he added, "Some-load-yagotthere," nodding and chuckling, but he commented no further. Walking down the aisle, I felt like everyone was staring at me as I alternately hoisted the two bags over the seats, careful not to hit anyone in the head. I was grateful that Shannon was walking ahead of me, as she always did, until I realized she was making her way all the way to the back of the bus. This was an area to which I had never ventured, until the high schoolers switched buses and the younger kids darted back to wrestle each other for the seats farthest from the front. "Shannon," I hissed, nudging her in the lower back with her bag as she passed the empty seat I always grabbed for Lori and me.

"Watch the ribs," she said through her teeth while smiling at her friends and giving them a beauty pageant wave.

I kept my head down, embarrassed to face Shannon's friends,

but was grateful when Becky reached out to take Shannon's bag. I hurried to the front of the bus and made it to my seat just as Mel opened his accordion doors and said, "H-hi, Lori."

This went on, painlessly, for the next couple of weeks, until I was given the horrible news: We were changing buses. I was offered no explanation why, but I knew I was not to ask, because it had something to do with Ted riding our bus. I had noticed, too, that lately Shannon's friends had not seemed as eager to greet her. In fact, some of them whispered or snickered now as she took her seat.

Again, I tried to argue. "But I don't know anyone on that bus!"

"It's only temporary," Mom tried to explain.

But I could not imagine surviving such a thing for even a short time. How would I start each day without comparing outfits and planning flirting strategies with Lori? How could I compete in the "who can eat the grossest thing" contest, which I had won the previous year by scraping my teeth across a scum-soaked Drumstick wrapper I had pulled out of the garbage? How would I ever re-earn my place in the second-to-last seat, surrounded by seventh graders? If I left now, not only could I lose my position as a Cool Fest officer, but I could be thrown out of the group altogether.

I was convinced Shannon was doing this to me on purpose. After all, weeks of physical therapy had gone by, so I could not understand how she wasn't getting better. I suspected she was feigning her helplessness, not to get out of carrying her own bag, but to get out of doing all of the housework that was now solely my responsibility. My new chores, and my refusal to do them, were the cause of most of my arguments with Mom and Dad, which resulted in my being grounded more often than not. Because there wasn't much to do outside of school, being grounded meant being unable to spend the night at Lori or Sheilah's house. If I really misbehaved—like the time I hurled a stool through my bedroom wall rather than feed the dog—I was also barred from the phone, a fairly useless punishment, as Mom was always on it.

After a while, getting grounded became so commonplace that my defiance became something of a sport. I kept my room fairly clean but refused to touch the rest of the house, only touring it from time to time to point out other peoples' messes: Dad's countless dirty dishes, Mom's overflowing ashtrays, Shannon's scattering of beauty products, Corey's weightlifting equipment, and Neil's abandoned toys. I took every opportunity to point out the injustice of me, who spent all the time I wasn't grounded away from home, and all the time I was grounded in my room, being asked to clean.

On the occasion that I had very important plans, like attending a co-ed birthday party that would involve Truth or Dare, I would do the chores, but make an obnoxious display of my disgruntlement. Once when I had broken a dish on purpose, Mom made me scrub the stove.

"Why doesn't *she* ever have to do anything!" I screamed at the top of my lungs, glaring directly at Shannon, who was sitting in the living room with Mom and Dad watching TV.

There was no response, so I began swiping the spilled spaghetti noodles and unpopped popcorn off of the stove and onto the floor.

Mom, hearing the kernels skip and the spaghetti scatter, calmly stated, "Okay, now I guess you're sweeping the floor, too."

"No, I'm not!" By now I'd worked myself up to a pant. "Can't you see she's just faking it! She can lift her stupid crimping iron every morning, so I think she can lift a plate. Of course, maybe she doesn't know how, since she never eats!"

"You go to your room right now!" Mom said, jerking her head up and baring the whites above and below her irises, which was my sign she had had enough. I thought she was going to come after me, but she didn't. She just put her head into her hands and shook it.

Finally, Dad spoke up. "Get to your goddamn room," he said with disgust.

I heard a sniffle and realized it was coming from Shannon, who was biting her bottom lip and staring at the floor. Her face was blotchy like Spike's had been, when she found out Mom was pregnant with Neil, but she carried none of the arrogance. Nor did she have the glow of a post-ball Cinderella. Instead, she looked like a sad, crippled old lady.

"Now!" Dad said, angrier.

I had no comeback, so I looked at the floor, at the mess that I'd just made.

Non-African Queen

Each Labor Day weekend, the nearby metropolis of Prentice (population 641) broke out all of its finery—its fire truck, a horseshoe set, half a dozen picnic tables, enough flags to line the parade route—to celebrate Prentice Progress Days, a festival that, like the town itself, never advanced. The softball game, bake sale, and log-loading contest drew good crowds every year, but it was only the Miss Prentice coronation that succeeded in luring residents away from the beer stand.

In the weeks leading up to the event, I had been approached by several local business owners wanting to sponsor me in the competition. Six of my friends—with whom I'd been getting reacquainted—were already practicing their waves and acceptance tears. They encouraged me to enter, but it was only when I learned that my archenemy Tara had entered that I threw my tiara in the ring.

Tara was the stuff beauty pageants were made of: shiny blonde hair styled by her hairdresser mother, blue-green eyes, and a dazzling smile. We had succeeded in turning anything into a competition: boys, clothes, extracurricular activities. Even our eating disorders.

"We'll take her in the question and answer portion," Sara said confidently, after squealing over my news.

"Yeah, piece of cake," I said. "But she's got the home court advantage over me in the parade."

"Yeah, but you've got bigger boobs." I did not take this as a compliment and made a mental note to forgo the yogurt I had planned to indulge in the next day.

I spent the morning of the competition under a hair dryer. My sponsor, Tara's mother's competing beauty salon, turned my fine hair "Texas," with teased roots, sky-high bangs, and rhinestone-encrusted floral sprays that peeked out from under a lacquered French twist that would take days to wash out.

"Don't get ass dents in my car," a friend's boyfriend said as I carefully mounted the back of his red Iroc convertible. My sponsor had neglected to tell me that the car would clash with my dress, which was fuchsia with three tiers, a large rhinestone-encrusted bow, and an overlay of black lace. I had matching gloves and pointy high-heeled pumps, which I had agreed not to wear when stepping on the leather backseat.

For the entire length of Main Street (which consisted of a few taverns, a fire station, and a used car lot), I waved just like I had practiced years earlier in anticipation of my royal wedding. The only thing that resembled my fantasy, however, was the condition of the revelers' teeth, as those living in England and northern Wisconsin were equally notorious for their lack of oral hygiene. Instead of roses, they tossed catcalls and sick come-ons at me. I rode not behind a motorcade, but a tractor from a local implement store. I couldn't even see Tara, as the jacked-up pickup that was two car lengths ahead of me blocked my view. When the parade ended, friends who had watched from the crowded sidewalks assured me I looked much more "princessy" than her, giving me a boost of confidence for what was reputedly the hardest phase of the competition, the question and answer session, in which each of us greeted the judges alone. Previous contestants warned me that the judges were ruthless and that I should be sure to wear waterproof mascara in case I cried.

If they were bulldogs, the judges didn't show it. They sat at a lunch table that had been carted into the high-school English room. The home ec teacher, who was obviously their leader, wore a dress with a doily collar. The women who sat next to her, each looking like her clone, smiled pleasantly and sat with their hands and ankles crossed. I was first asked to introduce myself, which I was told is where most girls botched their chances. Then they asked me about my extracurricular activities. I regaled them with stories about forensics, playing the lead in the school plays, and my leadership roles in class government and any club offering the chance to be president. In response to their final question—"Who is your role model, hon, and why?"—I dealt Tara a final death blow: "Though I'm inspired by my mother and her mother before her, I see in Katherine Hepburn a spirit that encourages women of all ages, including me, to be their best selves." Little did they know that my exposure to Katherine Hepburn had been limited to Martin Short's parodies of her on *Saturday Night Live*; I figured if she was important enough to share the stage with The Church Lady, she was significant enough to qualify as role model material.

The coronation took place in the church parking lot. One by one, my fellow contestants and I mounted the rickety risers that were set up on the handicapped parking spot. I eyed my competition. Sara winked at me. A heavy classmate wearing a peach and white lace gown twirled her matching parasol. Tara stared straight ahead, her posture perfect.

The emcee was the president of the Lion's Club, a man apparently past his prime in everything but telling lame one-liners. As he droned on and on, I looked into the crowd, noting which of the college boys who were home for the holiday were checking me out. I looked for Natalie but could not find her.

When the third runner-up was named, we clapped our gloved hands politely, quietly thanking God we weren't in fourth place. Third place went to a nice girl who was rarely singled out for anything. I was genuinely happy for Sara, who took the second place title. If, for any reason, Miss Prentice were unable to uphold her duties—duties with which none of us was familiar—the crown would pass to her.

Now only Tara and I remained of the crowd favorites. As we stepped together to fill in the gap left by Sara, I wondered if we should make a good show and clasp hands like the final two contestants for Miss America. I didn't even have a chance to reach for her hand, as suddenly girls were throwing their arms around me and pelting me with kisses. The tiara—which had five rhinestone hearts, each with a dangling teardrop-shaped rhinestone in the center—was placed on my head by a girl who had a shiny green dress with two tiers and a black lace overlay. A photographer for *The Bee* captured the moment in a photo that would appear on next Tuesday's front page. In it, I stood in front of the Prentice Volunteer Fire Department ambulance holding a dozen roses and wearing a sash with gold stick-on letters that would later peel off in my hair and declare me MISS P EN ICE. My smile revealed that I had no idea what was to come: dozens of parades in towns every bit as crummy as Prentice.

I completed the majority of my required appearances, telling myself to hang in there just a bit longer. Then I got a sign: my tiara flew off at a country fair and was crushed by a moster truck. The next step on the circuit was Miss Northwoods, the qualifying pageant for Miss Wisconsin. I knew my competition—among them a pie-faced violinist, a chubby aspiring veterinarian, and a girl who used to eat her boogers at Girl Scout camp—and knew there was a very good chance I'd get struck representing The Dairy State in the Miss America pageant. I forfeited my title, certain that Katherine Hepburn, or at the very least Martin Short, would have approved of this, my first and last royal decree.

Miss Prentice

Natalie, age 14

It was Prentice Progress Days, which I usually enjoyed like a distasteful joke; this year, however, I took it very seriously, and my presence was extremely important. Erick would be there. I didn't really know Erick, but I had seen him the previous year skateboarding with my friend Chris, who lived in Prentice but, unlike Erick, had gone to my school in seventh grade. I had first noticed Erick's hair, unlike any kid's at my school—short in the back and longer in the front, with a silky brush that swished over one eye as he shimmied across the pavement. Then I noticed his cute upturned nose and his plump lips. And then he smiled. It was too good to be true—Erick had braces! Although I had outgrown my infatuation with Mikey, I was still fascinated by the metal mouthpieces. Now, after Chris informed me that his best friend liked me, I hoped my chance to taste them would finally come.

I hadn't kissed Erick yet, but the night before, we had shared a very special moment. It was at the annual eighth-grade dance at the VFW hall. After watching Erick for hours goofing around with his friends during the fast songs and sitting on the bench alone during the slow ones, I approached him and asked him to dance. I was expecting to be shot down quickly and harshly; despite Chris' reassurances and my impressive record when it came to boys, I thought Erick was *way* too cool for me. He did say no, but I was surprised to discover that Erick was actually friendly. He even seemed a little nervous talking to me. After much begging on my part, Erick finally admitted the reason he didn't want to dance with me: He had never slow-danced before. "I don't care. I'll teach you," I said. After a few more nos, Erick slowly rose. "God, I can't believe I'm doing this," he said, shuffling to a spot three feet from the bench.

He looked at the floor the whole time, but he was not a bad dancer. We sat together for the rest of the night, and I did most of the talking, focusing on the things we had in common. After exhausting the topics of school and Chris, I started making fun of the other kids at the dance, since I knew, based on Erick's conversations I had overheard, that this was one of his hobbies. He laughed at my insults and added some of his own. Maybe we *would* make a good couple, I thought. Just as I seemed to be making an impact, Erick said he had to leave, because his parents were expecting him home early. I was disappointed, but when he mentioned he would be at Progress Days, I knew I'd have another chance to impress him.

So the next day, after ditching my family at the pageant I refused to watch, I scanned the crowd for Erick. He was nowhere to be seen, so I finally made my way to the rides: a creaking Ferris wheel, a giant red apple, and—my favorite—the salt & pepper shakers. Although I always came out of that ride with a sore neck and bumps on my head, it was by far the most exciting. There was no line, because everyone was at the stupid Miss Prentice ceremony, I speculated, but I decided to wait anyway. Although Erick's interest in me had heightened my confidence, and I was proud of walking the grounds alone, I could not bring myself to ride solo.

Finally, I saw a boy from school who was one of my admirers. Sam was nice and funny, but chubby and a little on the dorky side. Normally, I would be happy to see him and share a few laughs. But knowing that Erick could turn up any minute, I did my best to keep our conversation short. Sam was holding a small teddy bear. "Do you want this?" he asked. "I mean, I'm not giving it to you or anything. I won it and I think it's ugly, so you can have it if you want it."

Just as I reached out to inspect the stuffed animal, there was Erick, strolling toward the rides. "Sure," I said, snatching the bear without taking my eyes off of the object of my infatuation. "I guess I'll see ya later then," I said, having already slid past Sam.

Erick didn't see me right away, so I sat on the curb to wait. If he didn't approach me, I decided, the night before meant nothing to him and I would just have to accept that, as hard as it would be.

As he got closer, he slowed down, as if he didn't know what to do. I couldn't help but wave him over. An embarrassed smile flashed across his face, which he soon corrected. "Hey, what's that?" he asked, pointing at the bear. I showed it to him, and he took it out of my hands and began to make it dance across his lap. I laughed. "Since you like playing with it so much, do you want to keep it?"

"Do you really want me to?"

"Yeah."

"Are you sure?"

"Yeah."

Just as things were really getting good, we were interrupted by Jamie, another of Erick's Prentice friends. "Hey, guess who's the new Miss Prentice?" he said, looking at me.

Oh, no. "Who, Tara?"

"No . . ."

"Who? I don't even know who else is in it."

"Your sister."

Oh, great, I thought. Before, none of my peers seemed to notice Shannon was in the running, because it was considered uncool to watch the parade. Now, everyone would know. "Really?" I said, mock-shocked, as though I hadn't known Shannon was a contender.

Jamie nodded, smiling sinisterly.

"Oh, God," I said, exaggeratedly rolling my eyes.

Then, casually kicking a rock across the pavement, Erick opened his mouth. "She's not even *from* Prentice."

Now I was *really* embarrassed, not only because my sister was a boondocks beauty queen, but because *I* wasn't from Prentice, either. Though I attended Prentice Middle School this year, because Tripoli didn't have a middle school and Brantwood didn't have a school, period, I knew I'd never completely fit in. Though I had already befriended some of the Prentice boys, the Prentice girls—with whom I lumped the Ogema girls, bussed from another town similar to Prentice—were nothing like those from Brantwood and Tripoli. The Prentice and Ogema girls applied makeup and curled their hair even *before* gym class and basketball games. They seemed to be constantly whispering and talking about boys, and the boys seemed to like this. When I started school at Prentice, I was no longer popular and sought after among my classmates. I was just one of the boys.

I was determined not to be like these girls under any circumstances, but I sometimes wondered what kind of reception I would get if I covered up some of my blemishes, plucked my unibrow (as Mom and Shannon had long begged me to do), and ditched my perpetual uniboob. I even wondered what, in addition to wearing a sports bra only for sports, a more girlish wardrobe would do for my figure. Weeks before, when Shannon wasn't home, I had sneaked into her room and slipped her pageant dress off its hanger. I carefully stepped into the ring of ruffles, making sure my feet didn't touch the fabric, and slid the dress over my thighs. It was a tight squeeze, especially over my widening hips, and even tighter when I zipped it up. But the snug fit was a nice change from the extra-large T-shirts and sweat shorts I usually wore to school. My hair, a short mushroom-shaped cut, didn't quite fit the look, though, and I knew better than to try on Shannon's shoes.

As nice as it felt to wear a dress, I knew it would be a long while before I'd admit this to Mom and Shannon. I was determined to prove to them that I was good enough the way I was, as unsure of that as I was, myself. I feared that boys wouldn't like me for me, either, but apparently I was wrong because, the night after Progress Days, Chris called to ask me out—for Erick! I knew I would say yes, but I wanted Erick to ask me himself. Once Chris persuaded him to take the receiver, and after about an hour of small talk, Erick finally popped the question. Then Chris got back on the phone, and he sounded very upset. He confessed that he had planned to ask me out at the dance that night, but once he saw how much I liked Erick, he couldn't bring himself to do it. He said, "You have always been me and Erick's dream girl, except now Erick doesn't have to dream anymore." I felt bad for my friend, but I couldn't help being happy that I was *anyone's* dream girl.

Although it took what seemed like months to get Erick to kiss me, when he did—or rather, when I forced a kiss upon him—it was everything I had hoped for. His braces were, in fact, delicious, as were his juicy lips. Our conversations, which almost always took place in the form of notes, usually consisted of various loving sentiments and, more often, assorted questions and/or reassurances. The letters always ended with "Love Always," "Love Forever," or

"Love Always and Forever."

In one particularly special note, Erick wrote, among other things, "I want you to know that I will never dump you." I clutched that note to my chest and read and reread it every night before I went to bed.

Then, a couple of months later, this note came: "I don't think we should go out anymore." I was devastated, of course, but part of me knew this had to be a game, and I knew his reason, that our relationship was affecting his grades, could not be valid. If I was still getting As, thinking about nothing but him, how could his grades be suffering? I begged Erick to take me back, and he did. Things were better than ever, until he dumped me again, this time, he said, because he didn't know if he loved me anymore.

I cried all day at school, not caring—or rather hoping—that Erick saw me. He didn't seem too affected by my tears, and I even caught him laughing a few times, first with his friends, and then with the Prentice and Ogema girls. By the time school was over, my stomach was sick, and I spent most of the night in the bathroom throwing up what little food I had eaten at lunch. When I stepped into the hallway, I met Shannon on her way to her room. She asked me if I was okay and said she had heard, from someone at school, that Erick and I had broken up. "Breakups suck, I know," she added, her face serious and even a little sad. No words would come from my quivering lips. "Well, if you need someone to talk to, let me know," she said before disappearing into her room.

I went into my own room, dumbfounded by Shannon's offer

and her omission of the word "dumped." I collapsed onto the bed, and after bawling uncontrollably for several minutes, took a few gulps of air and focused on how I could get out of my forensics meet the next day. It would be difficult, because I was in a play with three other girls, and I knew *The Effect of Gamma Rays on Man-in-the-Moon Marigolds* would not be the same without the crazy mother. On top of having to face my friends' disappointment at my bailing on them, I would have to face Mr. Abney, who was not only my acting coach, but also Shannon's, whom he treated like a Hollywood starlet. He had even expressed once that he thought it must be difficult for me to live in Shannon's shadow. I had pretended I didn't know what he was talking about and then assured him I had no desire to be like her. In fact, I confessed, I had only joined forensics in the first place because all my friends had. Now, I considered using my tears to my advantage; yes, Shannon could cry in plays, but *her* tears were fake. As much as I wanted to prove I could act as well as Shannon, I couldn't imagine riding a bus with Erick and gaggles of giggling girls. Returning to the thought of Erick, I began to bawl again.

Not long after my bawling turned to sobs, Mom knocked on my door. I figured she had come to tell me all of the things that all mothers tell their heartbroken daughters: that they have their whole lives ahead of them; that this is not the end of the world; that there are other fish in the sea. When I didn't answer, she knocked again, this time opening the door a crack. "Yeah?" I coughed, sitting up in the dark. She opened the door and, surprisingly, didn't say anything. She didn't turn the light on, either. The room was uncomfortably silent, but for the creaking of my box spring when she lowered herself onto my bed. She just sat there for a while, gently sighing every time I hiccupped away my sobs. Then finally, she reached out and wrapped her arms around me. At first, it felt strange, because I couldn't remember the last time she had hugged me. Her body was warm and cushiony, and she smelled faintly of smoke, which, right now, didn't even bother me. "I know it's hard," she said, rubbing my back. I burst into tears again, not because of Erick but because my mom was hugging me and it felt good. I didn't exactly hug her back; my body didn't seem to know how. But I didn't push her away, either. Between my wails and shudders, I thought I heard her voice say something else, this time softer. It sounded like "I love you."

After she left, I continued to cry, not just about Erick but about everything—all I had lost, all I had gained, and all I hadn't realized was missing.

Black on White

A HALF-DOZEN GIRLS STOOD AROUND THE PIANO, nervously swaying in their stonewashed jeans rolled tight on the bottom. I was one of them, and we were all trying our best to sound just like Vanessa Williams. Her "Save the Best for Last" was the song we'd sing at our graduation, which was just a few weeks away.

When in regular choir practice, I usually entertained myself by belting out my own lyrics in full Tourette's syndrome fashion, or by purposely singing off-key to make the director feverishly scan the rows for the culprit, her heavily plucked eyebrows shimmying up and down her forehead. Today, I looked at my fellow songstresses and wondered if they were as scared as I was to leave the clammy brick walls of Prentice High.

Most of my classmates knew what their futures held. A few had already given birth to one or more children. Some were engaged. Some had taken jobs at the factory where their parents worked, and a handful had been accepted to state schools. I'd thought about moving to New York or Los Angeles to act, or going to a large university out east to study English (en route to winning my Oscar or Nobel peace prize).

Unfortunately, my parents hadn't been able to save for college—especially with my high medical bills, which would take them several more years to pay off—but I suspected their resistance to my ideas was more because they wanted me nearby. My weight had stabilized in recent months, and this was even more emotionally painful for me than the eating disorder itself. I'd struggled with relapses each time the numbers on the scale took a jump, and my parents' concern was, in truth, warranted.

When I received an application packet from one liberal arts college, however, there was no talking me out of my plans.

The brochure had a thick sage-colored cover with flecks in the paper. A window had been cut out, through which a glossy photo of the turret of an old building flanked by a flowering tree showed. I didn't even need to open the brochure to know that this was my school. I called the number listed on the back and asked about their programs and the cost of tuition. It was well over $20,000, but the woman on the other end of the phone assured me I'd qualify for scholarships. I did, and I enrolled.

"Will Corey be going with you?" Mom asked, her face full of hope that I'd say yes. The school was four hours from home, and I knew that for her, saying yes meant she would be able to sleep nights, knowing I'd eaten and gotten home safely.

"Yes," I answered. "We'll live off campus." Beyond this, I had no idea what my future with him would resemble.

Corey and I had been together three years now, and in a life that I'd worked so hard to fix, he'd come to symbolize all that had been broken. Abney and others had pointed out that we were "mismatched," and though I defended him endlessly, I knew deep down that we were. Corey had no plans to go to college, and he certainly had no intention of spending weekends on a sailboat, airplane, or any other craft that would take us far, far away from Brantwood. In fact, his goal was to eventually build a house on his family property, just a few miles away, and fill it with children. The attraction I'd once felt for Corey had by now mellowed into a fondness, and the more he talked about "our" future, the more afraid I became. When he started talking about marriage, I became petrified. "It only makes sense that that's the next step," Mom had said when Corey mentioned that we'd looked at rings after eating at a Mexican restaurant one night. I did find a ring I liked, with a curving band of gold and three tiny stones. It was far more than Corey could afford, but he began saving nonetheless. I thought it would take forever for him to earn enough, but I was wrong.

The night before my graduation, Corey dropped to his knee in my bedroom and offered me the ring. We'd just learned that cohabitation was not permitted on campus, and that all freshmen and sophomores not living at home or with a spouse had to live in the dorms. I felt trapped as I looked at his tanned face, and had trouble staring into his vibrant blue eyes. He looked like that new actor, Brad Pitt, the kind of guy someone should be happy to marry. But I cried as he slipped the ring on my finger, and I cried when we went to the living room to tell Mom and Dad the news. Neither of them suspected that the tears were not of happiness. After all, by the time they were my age, they had been married for a year and a half, and had just given birth to me.

I cried at graduation the following afternoon, too. As one by one, the kids I'd gone to school with for years, many of them since kindergarten, went to the stage to collect their diploma and red or white carnation, I mourned the past that was, and the future that might never be.

"Cold feet," everyone said when I confessed that I felt uneasy about getting married. "Everyone has them before the wedding."

Uneasy was actually an understatement. I'd been nauseated for weeks and couldn't sleep. Instead I lay awake at night, plotting various scenarios that would render me incapable of marriage: a serious-but-not-disfiguring accident, running away, our blood test revealing that we were siblings. But this sort of luck was for soap opera heroines and apparently not for me, because in the middle of August, three months after I'd graduated, and three weeks before college started, I found myself at the church, getting buttoned into my wedding dress.

"You look like you should be in a magazine," Sara, who was one of my bridesmaids, said, her eyes twinkling. I caught Natalie's eye, and she rolled her eyes, no doubt remembering my frequent childhood re-enactments of Princess Di's nuptial bliss.

It *was* a gorgeous dress. When I couldn't find the perfect gown, I'd sketched one (based on Julia Roberts' dress in *Steel Magnolias,* a role I played at the state forensics meet) and had it sewn by a local seamstress. Made of ivory silk, it had a fitted, off-the-shoulders bodice, a sweetheart neckline, and a full skirt covered by yards upon yards of tulle. As I looked at myself in the full-length mirror just before we headed to the lakeside park where the ceremony would be held, I got to thinking that maybe this wedding idea wasn't *so* bad. Corey had gotten his mullet cut off just for the occasion, and I was sure he'd look fantastic in his tux.

And then I walked past the wastebasket that stood near the door. Someone had thrown the copy machine's used ink toner cartridge in it, and the front of my skirt, which had apparently brushed against it while I was exiting the room, was now smeared with black ink. Sara shrieked. I felt the same stabbing in my ribs that came less frequently now. Even Natalie looked horrified.

"Okay, okay," said the lint roller-wielding, beehive-wearing seamstress who'd been warding off the threat of wrinkles all morning. "No one panic. We can take care of this." She took a few of the stickpins from the corner of her mouth and began gathering my dress into folds, and pinning the ink in the creases. Fifteen minutes later, I walked up the aisle to "The Wedding March" played by a harpist. The ink stains weren't visible, but I could not escape the fact that underneath its beautiful façade, my dress was irreparably flawed.

Uncle Jerry sang during the ceremony, which took place under a huge weeping willow tree beside a lake. As he performed "Heaven" by Bryan Adams, my mind wandered to Natalie and our younger years. When we were little, it had been only her and me. I turned to look at her, but she didn't look back. Wearing a dress, holding my flowers, she looked like a woman—poised, graceful, and confident even. When had she grown up, and when, precisely, had we grown apart?

Looking out into the audience, I saw people from every stage of my life looking back at me. Neil, now 6, looked adorable in his shorts suit, which had tails and was made from the same fabric as my dress. His eyes, framed by dark circles from the cold he'd caught the day before, showed deep concentration as he stared down at the rings on the satiny pillow in his hands. Mom, who feared she'd be too emotional to join Uncle Jerry, watched from the first row. She sat transfixed by Neil's legs, no doubt scanning for the first sign of a goose bump. Dad, who had surprised me with a limousine that morning, actually wore a suit. Gabby, in a vibrant blue dress that she'd bought new for the occasion, sat with her hands folded on her lap. They trembled slightly and were speckled with age spots. Papa sat beside her, the left corner of his mouth turned down in his version of a smile. Sonya's aunt wore a hairdo that looked pretty much like every other woman's her age. And then I spotted Mike, just as Uncle Jerry was entering the chorus. I had invited him but didn't think he'd really show. Mike's hair, longer than it had been when I'd last seen him, hung in his eyes, threatening to dip into the Marlboro that dangled from his mouth. He'd picked up stubble, a few pounds of muscle, and a girlfriend over the summer. She was one year our junior, an outgoing, smart girl with whom I'd acted. Throughout the song, she stroked Mike's forearm, to which he'd once pressed a hot lighter outside of my bedroom window when the jackknife he carried lost its allure. *What was I doing?*

When the music stopped, the minister, a woman from Grandma Kring's church, spoke.

"This morning, just before we all came here today, something happened that would have sent most brides into tears. But not Shannon. When I told Corey what had happened, and how Shannon had handled it with such grace, he said, 'That's my Shannon.'"

As she went on to talk about how it was this ability to remain positive in the face of challenges that would serve us well in our marriage, Corey squeezed my hands and looked into my eyes. His were filled with tears. I thought of all the love and support he'd given me over the years, and of how I wasn't able to give much in return. And then I thought of his words—"That's my Shannon"—and wondered how I could belong to someone else, anyone else, if I hadn't yet embraced myself. I didn't know how, but I vowed to find a way to right my wrongs.

I spent the rest of the day in a fog, Uncle Jerry documenting my every move with the refrigerator-sized video recorder hoisted on his shoulder. Here's what someone would see if they watched the footage: people—did anyone know them, or had they simply wandered into the pub in which the reception was held, looking for a cold one?—slopping two or even three helpings of Swedish meatballs, fried chicken, baked beans, and coleslaw onto chipped Corelle plates. Natalie, Lori, and Sheilah giggling and dancing "the Molly Ringwald." Old men in polyester suits watching young women's bluejean-clad asses as they danced (and the young women watching their own reflections in the Budweiser mirrors cluttering the banquet room's walls). A too-young bride flashing a too-big smile. A genuinely happy groom whose eyes wandered between said too-young bride and the door, through which he hoped his parents would enter (they didn't). Everyone drinking as if today was the day before Prohibition. All of this, with the sound-track of Garth Brooks crooning "I've Got Friends In Low Places."

Why Don't You
Ask Your Sister?

Natalie, age 14

"Why don't you ask your sister?" Mom proposed to
Shannon, who was struggling to decide upon whom to bestow the
exalted title maid of honor. They were standing in the kitchen,
where most of their wedding talk took place, and I was eavesdrop-
ping from the bathroom, where most of my phone conversations
took place. I had ended my call with Chris, whom I had recently
promoted from friend to boyfriend, but decided to hang around
and see where this conversation would go.

"Oh. I hadn't even thought of that." Shannon didn't sound too
excited by Mom's suggestion. So far, she had her candidates down
to Sara and Tammy. I may have been in the running for bridesmaid
no. 3, but I hadn't yet been informed.

"Just think about it, Shannon. That would solve the problem

of having to choose between your two best friends."

"Yeah, I guess . . ."

As I looked in the bathroom mirror, at my boyish mushroom haircut and overgrown eyebrows, I imagined what Shannon was probably thinking. I didn't have to imagine for long.

"But what would we do with her hair? And how would we get her to wear makeup?"

"I don't know, curl it?" Mom apparently agreed with the makeup part.

I could take no more; I decided to make my entrance.

"Hey, Natalie," Mom said, "what would you think of being in Shannon's wedding?"

"I don't know. I guess I could," I said, kicking myself for not utilizing a pause to indicate thought.

"And what if you were maid of honor?"

"I don't know. What would I have to do?"

"Oh, not too much. Help her get ready, adjust her train for pictures . . . I think the other girls would take care of the rest. I'm sure they realize you're younger . . ."

"And you'd have to wear makeup," Shannon interrupted. "And do something with your hair," she said, eyeing it while scrunching her upper lip, as though she'd caught a whiff of meat cooking on a grill.

"That would look stupid," I insisted. "I'd look like Gabby."

"Well, you'll have a little time to grow it out before the wedding."

"I'm not growing it out."

Shannon puffed out an exaggerated sigh.

"We'll figure out something," Mom assured Shannon.

And figure out something they did. Weeks before the wedding, my hair had not grown to Shannon's desired length, so she curled it. After it still didn't meet her standards of femininity, she decided to plunk a pearl headband on my head. The pearls matched the cream base of my dress, which I had just tried on. I had recently learned from my home economics teacher, during a "color analysis" workshop, that cream "washed out" my "winter skin tone." White, the students had agreed when I'd held up two pieces of construction paper to my face, was much more flattering to my complexion. Shannon had chosen cream to match her dress, and I knew there was no changing that at this point. I also knew there was no erasing the giant roses and lilacs that patterned the dress, but I complained nonetheless. I even had a problem with the length of the skirt. Because I was at least six inches taller than the other bridesmaids, at the first fitting my hem came nearly to my knees, while theirs grazed their ankles.

At the wedding, I was both relieved and disappointed to discover that the main focus was not the design and disproportion of my dress or my horrible hair and uncharacteristic makeup, but the bride, my sister. Even as I hastily arranged her dress for pictures, Shannon nervously looking down at me, everyone's eyes were on her. I realized that this day, though more grandiose, was not unlike any other. I wasn't sure why Shannon was nervous, because it wasn't like her to feel uncomfortable in the spotlight. I had figured it was because she was afraid I would mess up her dress, but her smiling lips were twitching even after I had finished.

After I stepped back into the grossly uneven line of bridesmaids, whose dresses, at least, were of similar length (after adjustments had been made), Jerry began to sing. My eyes gazed past the rows of guests and found Chris, whom Shannon had surprisingly asked to be an usher, despite his flipped black bangs with bleached tips. Chris was from a close-knit Italian family. I imagined our wedding would be something like *The Godfather,* with half of these humble guests replaced by boisterous Italians dancing the tarantella, passing money-packed envelopes, and hugging and kissing with Roman abandon.

After the ceremony, I reluctantly took my place in the receiving line next to Shannon. The first to greet her was Sara's sister, who ran to Shannon with her arms outstretched. "Oh, my God! You look just like a princess!" she squealed, giving Shannon a tight, cheek-to-cheek hug.

As the line proceeded, and each person hugged Shannon, it occurred to me that perhaps I was supposed to do the same. I had watched with envy as Chris' family hugged at such occasions, and even at home for what seemed to be no reason at all. Once, his sister had greeted me with a hug, and I had not known how to react. Ever since, I began to take mental notes on how it was done. I looked over at Shannon, planning where I might place my arms, and determined that no position would be comfortable.

I then realized I had not even congratulated her or complimented her appearance, which everyone also seemed to be doing. I had never congratulated her for any of her achievements, so why should I congratulate her for this, I rationalized, which wasn't really an achievement, anyway. It was just an excuse to get things for her new apartment, I had told myself. If I was greedy, I could get things, too. Shannon did look nice, I had to admit, but I didn't know how to say it. I listened to what words others had selected, but none of them felt right on my tongue. "Beautiful" and "lovely" were not adjectives we used, and certainly not to describe each other.

Before the reception, I begged Mom to let me change into jeans, but she flat-out refused. "This is your sister's day," she stated, and walked away. I sulked a while, but once the lights started skipping across the dance floor, and the speakers began spurting music, I forgot about what I was wearing. My cousins, aunts, and friends were dancing, and I was not about to miss out. Once I got used to Jerry with his camcorder lurking in the background, I actually had fun, mimicking dances from '80s movies and urging others to do the same.

When I watched Jerry's tape alone the next day, I realized I hadn't looked all that bad. This time, I actually listened to the ceremony and teared up when Shannon said her vows. Although her smile had looked practiced, I decided, her words were sincere. The ceremony was beautiful, she was beautiful, and the dance was a blast. I would have told her all of this and more, if only she had asked.

ME WITHOUT YOU

THE FOG IN WHICH I SPENT MY WEDDING DAY
did not lift in the days following it. There I was, standing in the living
room on the day we were moving. Corey was carrying the last of our
belongings outside. Mom was sobbing. Dad was standing in the
doorway, nervously picking at his moustache. Neil's bottom lip
puffed in and out. And all I could do was stare down the hallway,
waiting for Natalie to come out and say goodbye. I wanted to give
her a hug, but when she finally emerged from her room, we mum-
bled "bye" with our heads down.

I don't remember the drive to our new apartment, only that it
didn't take long to unpack, as all of our possessions—a few pieces
of furniture, clothing, a TV, Corey's weight-lifting bench and dumb-
bells, my box of mementos—had fit in a small U-Haul trailer. When
we finished, Corey collapsed onto our new mauve and grey couch

with wood and brass trim. We had just purchased it with our wedding money, and he had carried it and the rest of our furniture by himself up the narrow staircase to our upper unit, as I was still afraid of re-injuring my ribs.

Though we hadn't yet made it to the grocery store, I went to the kitchen and opened the refrigerator. On the top shelf was a bottle of Champagne and two crystal glasses, with a note from the landlord that read "Congratulations on your marriage! Enjoy your new apartment!" I examined the wine label and wondered what Mom would think of my drinking alcohol. I put it back in the refrigerator and picked up the telephone.

Mom answered on the second ring.

"We made it."

"Oh, good." I could hear Dad in the background, asking if we'd made it. "How was the drive?"

"Long, but good," I said, realizing that if there was ever an emergency, we were 225 miles away.

"How's your apartment?"

"It's great," I said, opening the mauve blinds behind the stove to see outside. The landlords, who lived downstairs with their two small sons, had the lawn beautifully landscaped with Black-Eyed Susans, rose bushes, and tall grasses that bowed to the cushiony grass. After looking at several apartments with grime-streaked walls and exposed pipes, we were so happy to have found this one. Newly refinished, it had two sun-filled bedrooms and roof access and was eleven blocks from the Lake Michigan shoreline.

(In letters to my friends, however, I described the roof as a balcony and the location as "overlooking the lake.") In my excitement, it didn't occur to me that the landlords wouldn't want us as tenants.

"Yeah, you know," the landlady had said slowly when I'd called to check the status of our application. "You're really nice kids, and I'm sure you'd be good tenants. But we're really looking for someone older to rent the place."

"We don't drink or have parties or anything," I said. "I'll be busy with my studies, and—"

"That's not what I mean, Sharon."

"Shannon."

"Shannon. I mean, you're a very young couple, and we had it once before that we rented the place out to a young couple, and they split, and then we had to find new tenants. It's such a hassle going through placing ads, checking references, and all that."

"Well, you don't have to worry about us!" I said, sounding as chipper as possible. "We've been together four years already." It took a second phone call, but I finally convinced the woman to take us.

Now, talking to Mom, I could hear Natalie in the background then, asking Mom what was for dinner. I imagined what was happening at home, or rather at my *old* home, as this was now my residence. Neil was no doubt playing Nintendo, gyrating to the Teenage Mutant Ninja Turtles' rhythmic punches and kicks. Dad was likely watching the news with the volume full blast, as years of screaming chainsaws had taken a toll on his hearing. Everything, I was certain, was a noisy, messy flurry of activity that stood in stark contrast to the silent order of my apartment. Life went on without me.

"I'm on with your sister," Mom said to her.

"Oh, great. I guess we won't be eating until midnight," Natalie grumbled after an exaggerated huff.

"I have to go out and get something to eat yet," I said to Mom. I'd been making an effort to eat every day and was now up to a size five. I'd planned to try my hand at making spaghetti that night. "All we have is a bottle of Champagne. The landlord left it for us, with a card." I waited to see how Mom would react.

"Oh, that was nice of them."

I kept forgetting that I was an adult now.

I was nervous that I wouldn't be able to find the college and left extra early on my first day of school. I hadn't been driving long, as I wouldn't be caught dead navigating Cug's equally embarrassing successor back home and therefore didn't get my license until the week of graduation. Corey and I had just taken out a loan to get me a 1992 Chevrolet Cavalier, and though it was not the convertible I'd wanted, it was a newer car than I'd ever driven, and I was more nervous to drive it than I was to start college. By the time I drove the seven miles to campus, my neck and ribs were killing me.

I found the student lot, which was just behind the men's dorm. I watched two tall guys—basketball players, no doubt—

come from the front entrance. They wore keycards on cords around their necks and were checking out two girls, also wearing keycards, who stood in the walkway, examining a campus map. I looked down at my wedding ring and wondered, as I had so many times in recent weeks, what the other students would think of my being married already. I twisted the ring around, so that the tiny diamonds didn't show, and stretched my arm out in front of me. It could have been any ring, really. Then I thought of the silent vow I'd taken on my wedding day, and of Corey and his nerves of facing his first day at his new carpentry job, and turned the ring back around.

My first class, freshman honors—a special class for the top-scoring applicants, in which we'd read books and debate their merit, as well as the merit of everything and everyone else—was in Old Main, the building pictured on the brochure. It had ivy crawling up one side and, like the rest of the campus, resembled the East Coast schools I'd seen on TV. (Well, with the exception of the corn-field and sagging barn across the road.)

I found my classroom—a dark, wood-paneled room filled with bookcases—and took a seat at the long, wooden table in the room's center. The dozen or so students busied themselves with digging through book bags and arranging their pens and note-books, so as not to have to say more than a nervous hello to the person sitting next to them.

The professor, wearing a corduroy jacket, suede shoes, and a huge smile, entered the room. He looked like an older, more normal-weight version of Abney.

Smoothing the few strands of brownish hair he had combed over his bald spot, he addressed us. "Welcome, welcome, everyone! I'm so happy to see all of you here today. I'm Rev, the campus chaplain, and well, you're the top of the top, the students who placed highest on the entrance exams. Congratulations. You should be very proud of yourselves."

The rest of the class period passed quickly, as we went around the table, introducing ourselves. My classmates had come from larger schools and, judging by their hobbies—equestrian competitions, tennis, and the symphony—far different socioeconomic backgrounds than I had. I dreaded my turn, which was the sort of thing I used to live for.

"All right, Shannon . . . Shannon, you've got quite a last name, here," said Rev, shining his smile on me.

I felt my face redden. Against the advice of everyone I didn't ask, I had kept my name and added Corey's long Germanic name, forgoing a hyphen.

"Yes, it's a mouthful. Well, I come from—"

"What kind of name is that?" Rev interrupted.

"It's my husband's last name, actually."

Silence. All eyes were on me.

"You're married?" asked the girl, also named Shannon, who sat kitty-corner from me. I suspected that she had been the most popular girl in her high school, as well.

"Yes," I said, burning up.

"Wow, that's, uh, that's quite... That's a..." Rev stammered.

"What did your parents have to say about that?" Shannon asked, her blue-green eyes wide.

"They were . . . totally supportive of it, actually," I said, not wanting to elaborate. *Why hadn't I turned my ring around? Kept my maiden name, like I'd wanted to?*

"My parents would absolutely *kill* me," Shannon blurted to the nods and uh-huhs of the rest of our classmates.

By the time Rev got around to asking me what my parents did for a living, I had no shame left in me and told the truth. When I had finished, I looked around the table. Everyone had the same expression that they'd worn before. Telling the truth hadn't been as traumatic as I had imagined it would be. It actually felt good.

Despite my difference in background and marital status, I became extremely close with my classmates. For the first time in my life, I was a standout among standouts. I wasn't the best at everything, but here, it seemed, there was enough attention to go around. For once, some attention was enough.

Together, my peers and I waded through Schweitzer and Hemingway and struck up heated debates even outside of the classroom. At the end of class, as I watched them walk back to their dorms and I walked to my car, I was sad that my college experience was done for the day. At home, I'd excitedly tell Corey what I'd written about in expository writing or about something that had happened in the library that day. He, looking exhausted, would reciprocate by telling me about whatever he'd sawed, nailed, or sanded that day. As I got deeper into my studies, our common ground seemed to erode. By the time I became involved in extracurricular activities, I didn't care as much as I should have.

About two months into my first semester, I set foot in the female dorm for the first time. Four girls from honors and I took a seat at the piano in the lounge, which resembled the common area on *The Facts of Life,* complete with a laugh track produced by other freshmen, who sat over thick textbooks or watched music videos on the TV that hung from the ceiling.

The other Shannon began playing "The Piano Man," and the rest of us sang as loudly as we could. This time, I sang in tune, and all the right words.

Afterward, Trina, a tall, religious girl from out west, said, "I really miss my sister. You should hear her play piano. Don't you miss your sister, Jackie?" she asked the girl who was playing chopsticks with two fingers. They lived on the same floor.

"Gosh, yes," she said. "We talk every night, practically. She's the one who sent me this bracelet," she said, flashing the golden chain at us. I couldn't imagine Natalie giving me anything but an insult.

"What about you, Shannon?" Trina asked, looking at me. "I'll bet you and your sister rack up the phone bills."

"Yeah," I lied. "Almost every night."

"I wish I had a sister," said Shannon, who sighed and then began pounding out another song. It was dark outside now, and groups of girls began packing away their work and heading to the cafeteria.

"Hey, I've got to get going," I said, picking up my bag.

"Not already! You can come over and eat with us tonight. It's taco night! Mmmm, tacos!" Trina said, rubbing her stomach. Tacos did sound good. With Corey's modest salary and the small amount I made from tutoring and grading papers in the English and writing departments, we were barely able to pay our bills, much less buy groceries. More often than not, Corey ate chicken for dinner (which he didn't mind, as it was good for his muscles). A vegetarian for four years now, I usually ate a bagel.

"Nah, I've really got to go," I said.

"She's got a husband to get home to," Shannon reminded us all.

The entire drive home, I thought about Natalie. In truth, I hadn't talked to her since I had moved. Not because I didn't want to, but because I didn't know what to say.

The past few years, we'd certainly grown apart, but until now, I didn't realize the role she still played in my life. Somehow, it seemed, I knew myself only in relation to her. The outgoing one. The ungraceful one. The dreamer. I hadn't realized just how desperately I had sometimes wanted to switch roles. Did she ever long to be the center of attention, or the fearless one? I'd have liked to have listened rather than spoken, or to have taken a dance class. Most of all, I sometimes wanted to escape everyone's watchful eye. But there was already a sister for that role. And now that we were apart, what was my place?

Though I didn't dare step into Natalie's territory, it seemed she had no problem entering mine. When Corey and I went home for the holidays, I found her changed. Sure, she was still argumentative, but she carried herself differently. Her hair looked as though she'd curled it, and when we went out in public, she wasn't her usual meek self, but the boisterous girl I had been. She'd even become involved in clubs and student government at school, and she'd won an essay contest in which her English teacher had entered her. More surprising than her comfort with having her work appear in the newspaper was the bold stance she took against prayer in schools in the piece. Mom said she'd gotten some hate mail, but Natalie had seemed as unfazed by this as she was by the glowing letters she'd gotten from out of state. I was editor-in-chief of the college newspaper and wrote a column, but I forewent controversial topics in favor of pieces about creative uses for a worn-out Wonder Bra and the stages of the committed college man. Was this because I had a penchant for humor, or because I lacked the courage to say what I really believed?

Even Natalie's attitude toward me seemed to have changed. Though she didn't greet me the minute I got there, she did come out of her room shortly after I had arrived, and she didn't throw a tantrum when Mom told me to put my stuff in her room. I wanted to tell her I was proud of her for her award, but I lacked the nerve for such a thing. The rest of my visit, we were apathetic toward one another, which was, I supposed, a step in the right direction.

By spring, Corey and I had grown farther apart. I tried to include him in events at school, but he said he had no interest in hanging out with "college snobs." When that excuse failed, he said he didn't have anything appropriate to wear, so I bought him a nice dress shirt and vest. He looked great in it, very Brandon Walsh of *Beverly Hills 90210*, but couldn't wear it without tugging uncomfortably at the collar. No doubt because of my having picked up a psychology major, I came to view the ensemble as symbolic of our marriage, of all that didn't fit no matter how hard we tried to make it.

But that did not stop me from trying. I tried to be "wifey" in my every action: washing Corey's work clothes in our secondhand washer and then carting them down to the Laundromat on the corner, where I'd dry them when we had enough change. Whipping him up a protein shake in the blender Shirley had gotten us for our wedding. Unlacing his steel-toed boots when he got home at night. Packing him a lunch, which usually consisted of cold cuts on whatever spongy white bread was on sale at the neighborhood Kwik-Trip.

It was at an academic awards ceremony in the spring, which I attended alone, that I decided to give up. I looked across the banquet table at the beaming parents of my peers. I wished my parents had come. And no matter how hard I tried, I couldn't envision Corey and me sitting with our children like that someday. I couldn't imagine us having them in the first place. When I told him it was over, we sobbed together on the floor of our living room. My tears were heavy with guilt for having broken his heart, and with sadness for letting go of the past I had thought I wanted to forget, anyway.

I moved out before the end of the school year, tiptoeing down the stairs, so as to avoid the stares of the landlady, who I feared would say, "I told you so." By the end of summer, I had gotten used to living on campus. Dorm life wasn't exactly what I had imagined, as none of my visions included standing ankle-deep in someone else's shower water, or having to tape cheesy construction paper decorations on my door each time a holiday rolled around. But I enjoyed feeling a part of the campus community, and even took to dressing like my peers. Traipsing around campus in baggy sweatshirts and tattered leggings, I came to understand Natalie's present dress code (men's button-down shirts, tattered tennis shoes, and rummage sale bell-bottoms—and not from Angler's Lane, either). It was comfortable! When she came to visit with Mom, Dad, and Neil, I wondered if now people would be able to tell that we were sisters.

I was excited to have my family visit me "on the outside." For two years, I'd been describing to them what life was like in the real world, where teenagers said hello, rather than just expletives, to you, and where everyone—not just the Stevensons of the community—mowed their lawn. At last, I'd have a chance to show them the way, and to create positive memories of a family visit.

The previous spring, when I'd gotten a lead role in the school's production of *The Lion in Winter,* my family came to watch. It was the first time any of them had been to the school, and everyone, including Corey, got a new outfit for the occasion. After our curtain call, I collected my roses and rushed up to Corey, telling him that there was a wrap party at the campus bar.

"That sounds like fun," Dad said.

"Yeah, it will be," I said, waving to friends passing by. I gave Dad my apartment key and dashed out the door.

The party was fun, and even Corey seemed to enjoy himself. When we got home, Corey promptly went to the bedroom to change his sweater to a T-shirt. As I went looking for Mom and Dad, who were sitting quietly in front of the television, I noted the empty soda cans littering our new coffee table (which Corey had scored on a job and I had repainted to match the furniture), and Dad's snuff running down the side of the kitchen trashcan. I straightened up and then went into the bathroom to wash off my stage makeup. Seeing that my new hand towels—which were expensive and just for show—had not only been used, but left on the floor, I stormed into the living room.

"Who did this to my hand towels?" I demanded.

No one answered.

"I said, who did this to my hand towels? You don't just leave things on the floor at my house!" I chided. Usually, I was quiet in the apartment, even walking on the balls of my feet when wearing heels, so as to make a good impression on the landlords.

"Listen to yourself!" Mom said, sounding more sad than angry. "We come all this way, spending money we don't have, and this is how you act?"

"Did it ever dawn on you, Shannon," Dad asked, "that we would have wanted to come to your party with you?"

Until then, it hadn't. If I'd wanted to, I wouldn't have even known how to blend my old life with the new me.

Now after touring them around the campus, which they hadn't really seen on the previous visit, I left Mom, Dad, and Neil in my room. I took Natalie up and down my floor, introducing her to my friends. At first she seemed uncomfortable, but by the time we reached the last door, she appeared relaxed and almost happy. When I asked if she wanted to go see a movie—a request I'd rehearsed all morning—she said yes.

Eric, the guy I had recently started seeing, met us in the lobby of the theatre. I introduced him to Natalie, and they shook hands.

"Did you like the movie?" I asked her after we'd said goodbye to Eric and were leaving the theatre.

"Yeah," she said.

"Funny my friend Eric was there," I said, glancing at her to see if she had called my bluff, both on the meeting being accidental and on his just being my friend. She didn't reply. "Hey, Nat, maybe don't mention to Mom and Dad that you met him, okay." I knew that they would think it was too soon to become involved with someone else.

"Okay," she said with a knowing smile. It had been years since we'd shared a secret.

As we drove off together, I realized how different this visit, away from our childhood home and the roles we couldn't seem to stop falling into there, had felt from all the others. It felt as close to sisterhood as we'd ever come.

Homecoming

Natalie, age 20

It was Fourth of July weekend, and I was going home. It had been only two years since I'd left home for college, but turning down County Road D in my new-used Pontiac Le Mans, it seemed like it had been centuries. The lush green forests I had remembered from my childhood now looked slate-like and sparse, almost prehistoric. The shed at the end of D, on which was once written in red paint "The Blood of Jesus was Shed for You and Me," had seemingly disappeared into thin air or risen to the heavens. The house next to it that had been inhabited even after a fire had burned the second floor to cinders (a tarp became the roof), was also gone. Passing the scattered houses that followed, they too looked different. Or had they always been that way? Gray and splintered, yards littered with beer cans and junk cars. I remembered our yard's own centerpiece, The Cug Mobile. Had the car been a person, Cug would have been a perfectly fitting name—small, ugly, and odd. The car I was driving now looked almost identical, even down to the color. Although mine was white, it was covered in dust and mud. I had not been to a carwash since I'd bought the car, partially because all of my quarters were reserved for laundry and partially because I feared the suffocating garages and giant gyrating brushes.

I was now officially an adult, but there were still *a lot* of things I hadn't done. It was a wonder that I ever left home at all; as much as I had hated my home life as an adolescent, my fear of the outside world could very well have kept me there forever. Had I not found a small university, not much larger than my high school had been, and a boyfriend who was willing to go there with me, I doubt I would have made the move. My parents were not thrilled with my choice of a school; it was too far away—all the way across the state—and if I insisted on going that distance, they added, then I might as well choose a better university. (Although it had later proven to be a good school, my university's entrance requirements were lower than many of the other schools we had looked at, and my high school grade point average far exceeded their minimum.) But large schools, like those I'd seen on television, were far too intimidating, and the smaller area schools were too close to home. Plus, I was comforted by the knowledge that Matt was familiar with the city to which we were moving—in fact, it had been his hometown. Still, to my dismay, Matt could not be with me every second of every day. When he was at work, I would force myself to walk across the street to the library near my apartment, and I considered this quite a difficult feat. Although our neighborhood was very quiet and suburban, every time I ventured anywhere on foot, I imagined a murderer or rapist jumping from the shadows to attack me. Nor could I drive anywhere without Matt in the car to protect me from traffic—almost nonexistent in Brantwood—or carjackers, one of the many dangers Mom had warned me about on her frequent phone calls. In the years after leaving home, hyperventilation became my normal state of respiration. On this, my first solo road trip, it wasn't until I reached D that I could begin to breathe easily—until I remembered my destination.

When I arrived, Shannon was already there, her black Mercedes parked in the unpaved driveway at a safe distance from Dad's "woods truck." It looked out of place and uncomfortable, like a guest who had mistaken a barbecue for a black-tie affair. I parked on the road, hoping one of the motorcycles, three-wheelers, or four-wheelers whizzing by would accidentally smash into the "Mans" because I had finally decided to splurge on insurance.

I took a deep breath and opened the door. As I had suspected, Clyde was the first to greet me and danced sluggishly at my feet. Clyde was our obese golden retriever, who, despite his name and the masculine pronouns we used to refer to him, was actually female. We had adopted him from the humane society six years earlier, just days after our previous dog had run away. (To Dad's dismay, Mom insisted that all of our dogs—runaways and casualties of our gun-happy neighbor—were immediately replaced, which I now blamed for my hasty replacement of boyfriends.) After Neil cried over Mom's suggestion of getting a "girl dog," as it would be more likely to stay close to home, she told Neil that the docile golden retriever—with whom everyone else had already fallen in love—was a boy and let Neil name him Clyde, after his favorite basketball player, Clyde Drexler.

The transgender dog seemed to be the only one interested in my arrival. Mom, Dad, and Shannon were standing in the kitchen discussing Shannon's new job as director of marketing for an upscale resort—

"So then I get up to walk to the stage, and the governor leans over and says, 'See, that's what I'm talking about!'"

"Oh—Hey, Nat," Dad said, munching on cucumbers that were supposed to go in the salad. "Kerry, stop that!" Mom snapped, slapping his fingers. "OK, now go talk to your other daughter," she said, shooing him away. "Hi, Nat," Mom finally said, flashing me a tense grin. Hugs were still not customary in our family, which made greetings and departures awkward.

By now Clyde, too, was hovering around Shannon. "Nat, can you call him by you?" she pleaded, frantically brushing orange fur off of her floor-length fitted black dress. I looked down at my faded tank top and jeans, which were already covered in Clyde's slobber. "Come here, Clydey, Shannon doesn't like you."

Dad followed behind, a half-eaten tomato dripping juice into his hand. "So, Nat, what's new?"

"Umm . . . not much. I got all As again this semester . . ." I failed to mention the A- I had cried over for a week after receiving my grades and that I spent most nights awake, scanning papers for errors I may have missed in my previous ten revisions, or fabricating ridiculous plans for retrieving imperfect papers I had already turned in.

"Yep, yep," Dad said between crunches, "I knew ya would." For our parents, good grades had always been expected, not rewarded. Though I later realized their quietly confident, hands-off attitude helped me to excel academically and learn for the sake of learning, I had always secretly envied the kids who were rewarded with money for each passing grade.

If my grades did not earn me excessive praise, then my recently acquired job as a cashier at Shopko was not worth mentioning at all. Its only merit was that I had finally worked up the courage to enter the workforce. Actually, I didn't have much of a choice. My financial aid was dwindling, credit card bills were piling up, and Mom and Dad, though they helped out whenever they could, were not much better off than I was. I still got sick each day before work and spent my breaks in the bathroom to avoid the peopled break room, but I felt a slight sense of pride for having mustered the guts to get the job in the first place. Pride at such a minor accomplishment was not something I was willing to admit, especially after Shannon's boasting of actual achievements.

After dinner, a veggie dog for Shannon and brats and burgers for the rest of us, Shannon and I carried our luggage—my laundry basket and Shannon's large black suitcase and wardrobe bag—into Mom's writing room, where Shannon would sleep in privacy on the new futon. The couch would be my bed, as it had been on all of Shannon's visits while I was still living at home. Though the couch itself wasn't bad, I knew I would have to let Clyde in and out several times throughout the night, or put up with his constant barking and licking. On one of Shannon's visits, I had refused to give up my bed to her, screaming, "I don't know why you bother coming home, anyway. No one wants you here!" Of course, that wasn't true. Even I looked forward to her visits, until she arrived and all of the resentment of my childhood crept into my veins. My parents, who had grown more and more likeable each day I was away from home, seemed also to have fallen under her spell. Mom, slightly calmer these days, became overly anxious and overprotective; Dad, who had previously refused to worship any god, seemed to have found one in Shannon. Only Neil seemed unaffected. When we popped our heads into his room, on our way to drop off our luggage, he didn't so much as look up from his video game to greet us. He wasn't being rude. He was only being shy, as I understood all too well. I knew that within a few hours of our arrival, he would venture into the communal area and observe us at a distance.

"Nat, remember that?" Shannon said, pointing to the hole in Neil's wall.

"Yeah . . ." I replied, slightly embarrassed.

"What was that, a stool?"

"Yep." This time I let out a short laugh.

Opening the door to the writing room, which had at different times been both of our bedrooms, I noticed there was still a large gap and a jutting shard of wood between the side of the door and the frame. "Hey, didn't you do this?"

"Actually, I think Mom did, when she smashed the door in after I locked myself in."

After plopping our bags down, we decided to continue our temper tantrum tour, moving onto the kitchen. "Hey, look, there's still a grease stain on the ceiling!" I said, pointing excitedly, like Dad did when he spotted a rare bird.

"Remember that, Mom, when I flung a slice of pizza up there when you tried to force-feed me?" Shannon reminisced.

"Look, girls, I have one!" Dad chimed in, walking excitedly to the defaced cupboard, victim of a night's drunken outrage. By this time, we were all laughing, including Neil, who was peeking around the corner.

I looked over to the cupboard on the other side of the stove, the one that had once been Curly's apartment. "Hey, whatever happened to the Barbies?"

Shannon and I looked at Mom, whom we blamed for most misplaced items in the house. It had taken weeks of searching to find our baby books among the piles of decades-old rubbish in the cabinets under the snack bar. Though we knew she cared about us, Mom was not one to keep track of sentimental items or hang family pictures on the walls. If a stranger entered the house when no one was home, he/she would have no idea who the family was that lived there, except that they were very disorganized.

"Didn't we put that stuff up in the attic?" Mom surprised us.

Shannon grabbed a chair, put it under the entrance in the hallway ceiling, and looked to me. "Can you do it? It's so dirty up there." I hopped on the chair and hoisted up the panel. I could see nothing and knew better than to ask for a flashlight. Even if we had one, I knew the batteries would be dead. I groped around, expecting to feel cobwebs, or worse, a mouse corpse. Instead, I felt plastic. A garbage bag? I grabbed the corner and pulled it to the opening. It was heavy and bulky, how I imagined a body bag would be. I pulled it down and it fell to the floor with a thud, dust scattering over the carpet. "Oops. Sorry." No one but Shannon seemed to understand why I was apologizing.

I peeked through one of the small holes in the bag to see a chewed-up plastic arm. "Yep, it's them."

"Here, put it on the table," Shannon suggested, shoving aside a large heap of papers. I hoisted it up and tore open the bag. Now uncaring of her clothes, Shannon began tearing away the plastic, as if the mangled mass, mingled with mouse turds, had suddenly turned into a beautifully wrapped present. The tangled, lifeless body parts plunked, cluster by cluster, onto the table. Within seconds, Shannon spotted her. "Oh, my God! It's Rachel!" Shannon squealed, cradling her Malibu Barbie in her hands. I was delighted to see that Rachel's tan was now partially scraped off and that her golden locks were limp and lackluster. Surprisingly, this didn't seem to matter to Shannon.

I scanned the table for Tracy. "Here she is!" I held her up to Rachel. Now, they did not look all that different. We continued picking through the pile, stacking each of our Barbie collections in front of us, like we had done with our packages on Christmas morning. After we made our piles, we wrote down each name in our own separate columns—not to track who had more, but so that we would never forget them.

We continued writing, recording each character's personal history, occupation, temperament, fashion style, and more. Mom stood by speechless, either amazed by our remarkable imaginations, or maybe just shocked by our insanity.

When the document was done, I stared blankly at the page. Shannon must have noticed my expression drop. "What is it, Nat?"

It took what seemed minutes to formulate the words to express my horrible realization: "Oh, my God. We're becoming . . . our Barbies."

It had suddenly occurred to me that Shannon had become Rachel—superbly dressed, socially skilled, and wealthy by my standards. I, on the other hand, was plain in appearance, socially inept, and working for minimum wage. The only thing that separated me from Tracy was kids and a husband, which I figured I would someday too want and not have, or have and not want. I nearly began to cry.

"Oh, Nat, they're just Barbies," Mom attempted.

Shannon took another look at the page, not knowing what to

say. "God, I was horrible to you," she finally managed. It wasn't quite an apology, but it was an admission I had waited a long time to hear. I didn't know what to say, but I knew I was finally ready to bury the Barbies. Not just the dolls themselves, but also the blame and resentment I had carried with me all these years.

I could not say it that day, and maybe I didn't even realize it for some time, but I forgave Shannon for all of the torture she had put me and my Barbies through. After all, she was just a child—a child who dreamed big, but whose reality fell very short of her expectations. Looking around me, I realized it was natural for Shannon to make my Viskers poor and dysfunctional. It was also natural for her to want something better for herself, to create a fantasy world from what she had seen on TV, not from what she saw in her home and middle-of-nowhere community. And did I really want those things anyway, or did I want them just because Shannon had them? What did *I* want? It was a question I had been too scared to ask myself; it was so much easier to blame Shannon for my failures. I had no idea what would make me happy, but I knew that if I were ever to find out, I would have to put the past aside and begin to take responsibility for my own life.

On that day, I also accepted my Barbies—and my real family—for what they were. They were not rich and successful, but they were kind and smart and funny. They were not perfect, but I loved them all—Tracy, Wes, Katie; Mom, Dad, Neil—even Shannon. Maybe even myself.

Later that night, after everyone else had gone to bed, Shannon and I watched a movie, which, of course, she had picked out. It was a romantic comedy, too light and optimistic for my usual taste, but after an emotionally draining day, it seemed perfect. Despite our earlier bonding over Barbies, we sat at a distance from each other—Shannon on the chair with a bowl of unbuttered popcorn, and me on the couch with a bowl of buttered and a bag of Twizzlers.

"Gimme some lick," Shannon said, reaching out her hand. She apparently had given up on her diet. Though she'd recovered from anorexia, it had slowed her metabolism, so she was always watching her weight. She was also always "bloated," or claimed to be, no matter what time of the month I saw her.

"Ugh . . . I don't want to get up," I sighed. "Just come over here." I moved my legs to make room for Shannon, and she plopped down beside me. In Dad's sweats, with her makeup washed off, she looked a lot more like me. I handed her the bag of licorice. She took a piece and ate it just the way I did, alternating each bite with an equal portion of popcorn. "I shouldn't be caving like this, but I can't eat one without the other."

"Yep—you have to have both," I agreed. "A little salty, a little sweet."

ACKNOWLEDGEMENTS

I am indebted to the awe-inspiring sisterhood of women to which I am honored to belong:

The great poet Frances May, who—at 59 years my senior—recognized me as a writer and kindred spirit long before I wrote or uttered a single word in her presence. It is with great pride that I'll carry on her wisdom about life, love, and writing from a place of truth.

My Sheboygan Nia sisters, especially Lynn Gordon, who has danced with me through some of my most momentous life occasions, always leading with gentle wisdom and never once stepping on my toes.

My "holy trinity" of teachers: Jackie (Casey) Wendorf, my second grade teacher who encouraged my incessant writing and drawing, and who more than once turned a blind eye when I did it in my textbooks; the late June A. Dobbe, who taught me that there's nothing wrong with some "good, clean fun," and that a woman can be both strong and sensitive; and Martha Schott, who never once doused the flame of my grand plans.

The inimitable Lola Roeh, who gave my younger, cockier self her first break in business and a true taste of things to come. Her steadfast belief in life's limitless possibilities has guided my career and made me a better leader. I look forward to the day when we meet again.

My friends and life mentors, Dr. Deborah Kern and Mary Marcdante. Outstanding speakers, plain-truth writers, cheerleaders extraordinaire, these beautiful women inspired me to be the woman I am about to become. Thank you for all that you do for women everywhere.

The wise and inspiring Jean Reddemann (*Wasaki Emani Wi*, "Strong Walking Woman"), who has for the past nine years advised me on matters of business and the heart, and who has continually reminded me of my purpose. You will be with me as I step into the next phase of my life.

My closest spirit sisters, Coco Smith, a paragon of strength, friendship, and perseverance; Kate Ludwig, who has nourished my ever-evolving body and spirit; and Heather Blamey, who shines as an example of grace and all that is good. I cannot imagine my life without the three of you in it.

And especially my birth sister, Natalie, who it turns out wasn't so bad after all. In fact, even if this book does not sell a single copy, it's made me rich in ways that my childhood imagination could not fathom. I'm so glad you came into my life.

And I would be remiss if I didn't thank the men who helped make this book a reality:

Derek Degenhardt, who was the first to encourage me to write about my childhood, and whose wittiness has challenged me to be a better writer. My life and work is saltier and sweeter because of you.

The incomparable Karl Elder, who introduced me to the

grotesque (There was an ACTUAL NAME for what I wrote in college!), and whose tough love forged in me editing skills for which I'm grateful. Your grades meant something, as did your praise.

The resolute Marcel Biró, who has never once given up on me or in the potential of what we've co-created. Marcel, I would not be where I am today if it weren't for you, and I cannot wait to see where your wings carry you next.

—SHANNON

I would not have begun or completed this book were it not for the collective influence and encouragement of numerous mentors and friends. I would like to thank my early teachers; in particular, Ms. Debbie Gustafson, my eighth grade English teacher, the first to help me realize not only that I could write, but that I could *like* to write; Mr. Petrashek, the high school English teacher who sparked my infatuation with all things grammar, making editing easy and enjoyable ever since; and Mr. Abney, who gave me more writing experience and advice than I thought any history teacher should. My writing skills and interests were furthered by the English faculty at UW-Parkside, who gave me my love of literature, lots of practice with my pen, and invaluable suggestions for improvement. I am especially indebted to Julie King, who, through her ingenious exercises and relentless encouragement, helped me conquer my fear of creative writing; and Professor Carole Gottlieb Vopat, who helped me find a voice I didn't know I had, and for instilling in me the necessity of writing with honesty and dignity. I must also thank my other mentors, the former staff at Martha Merrell's Bookstore: Professor Andrew McLean, whose tough love has continually made me stronger; Kelly Voss, who—through example and praise—has done more for my confidence than she will ever know; and Ralph Schoenleben, who does not wish to be anyone's hero, but who is mine, nonetheless. Thanks to all of my co-workers for their enthusiasm and generous support, especially Jason Paul Collum, for—on numerous occasions—offering a bartender's ear and an artist's advice. My sincere gratitude to my employers at Out of the Pan, Jeannie Dillon and Roberta Schulz, for providing a flexible job that allows me ample time to write, and for doing more to promote my book than I have. I also thank my patrons, not only for their financial support, but for the genuine interest and excitement they have so kindly expressed. (Mortimer, Bob, Dan, Don, and the Susans—this one is for you. Pete, I thank you, too, for doing whatever it is that you do.) I thank my friends, too many to list them all by name, who have diligently diminished my doubts and provided much-needed diversions when my worries became overwhelming. In particular, I must thank the following: Bryan Wehr, one of my first "writing buddies," who was supportive of my work before I considered it work; Tina Wehr, who gave me much-needed perspective in the midst of my insanity; Jill Plaisted, who counseled me continually without a single complaint; Michele Skillings, who lent me her ear and also her memory stick (when I couldn't buy my own); Marc (Marcus) Riutta, who brought me laughter aplenty when I needed it most; Colleen Steenhagen, who has provided peaceful surroundings and peace of mind, time and time again; Steve Smith, whose faith in my abilities, when this book was little more than an idea, kept me pushing forward; Heather Wyrick, whose reminiscences proved beneficial to both my book and spirit; and Carl Hardy—late great storyteller and listener—who taught me that stories are not only essential to life, but that they are life itself. My deepest thanks to Guy Crucianelli, who stood beside me from the start; were it not for his steadfast support, relentless reassurances, and editing expertise (when I was ready to smash my pen to pieces), this book—and perhaps one of its authors—would not have made it to the end.

And Shannon, for continually converting my pessimism to optimism, and—through her boundless ambition— turning what I had considered an unreachable dream into a reality. Pushy, patient, salty, or sweet, I am proud to call her Sister and Friend.

—Natalie

We both wish to thank Bryon Zimmerman and Sherry Smies—two of our first supporters—for their generous praise and a killer proposal design; Lisa Clancy, our editor, for her fine work on our manuscript, and whose faith allowed us the autonomy to freely create; and Catherine Fowler, who far exceeded her obligations as a literary agent by reading and editing our manuscript in its numerous incarnations (and who proved herself a fine mediator, as well).

Obviously this book would not exist without our family: Dad, forever an example of humility and integrity, whose trust in our telling of this story means more than he could know; Mom, who instilled in us from an early age the importance of reading and writing, and whose extraordinary capacity for perseverance and self-creation has been our primary source of inspiration, both as writers and as women; our brother Neil, who despite his younger age, displays a quiet wisdom and dignity that far exceeds our own; and Uncle Jerry, whose ability to induce uproarious laughter even in the most somber of circumstances has strengthened our sensibilities and souls.

Finally, we would like to thank the supporting characters of our past—both in the book and out—who have colored our lives, created our stories, and shaped who we are today.

SHANNON KRING BIRÓ is the executive producer and co-star of the Emmy® Award-winning PBS reality cooking series *The Kitchens of Biró* and the co-author of *Biró: European-Inspired Cuisine, Johnsonville Big Taste of Sausage Cookbook,* and *SpanAsian Cuisine from Ó, a Biró Restaurant.* She co-owns two restaurants and a culinary school with celebrity chef Marcel Biró. Shannon is president of her own international restaurant and marketing consultancy. She lives in Sheboygan, Wisconsin, and Los Angeles, California. Please visit her at www.birointernationale.com.

Natalie Kring graduated Summa Cum Laude from the University of Wisconsin-Parkside. She is a published poet and former independent bookstore manager. She lives in Kenosha, Wisconsin.

www.sistersaltysistersweet.com